AN ILLUSTRATED HIST

SAINTS AND SAINTHOOD

AN ILLUSTRATED HISTORY OF
SAINTS AND SAINTHOOD

AN EXPLORATION OF THE LIVES AND WORKS OF CHRISTIAN SAINTS
AND THEIR PLACE IN TODAY'S CHURCH, SHOWN IN 200 IMAGES

TESSA PAUL • CONSULTANT: REVEREND RONALD CREIGHTON-JOBE

southwater

This edition is published by Southwater, an imprint of Anness Publishing Ltd, Blaby Road, Wigston, Leicestershire LE18 4SE

email: info@anness.com

web: www.southwater.com; www.annesspublishing.com

Anness Publishing has a new picture agency outlet for images for publishing, promotions or advertising. Please visit our website www.practicalpictures.com for more information.

Publisher: Joanna Lorenz
Editorial Director: Helen Sudell
Jacket Design: Nigel Partridge
Production Controller: Bessie Bai
Produced by Toucan Ltd:
Managing Director: Ellen Dupont
Editors: Malcolm Day, Anne McDowall
Designer: Elizabeth Healey

ETHICAL TRADING POLICY

Because of our ongoing ecological investment programme, you, as our customer, can have the pleasure and reassurance of knowing that a tree is being cultivated on your behalf to naturally replace the materials used to make the book you are holding. For further information about this scheme, go to www.annesspublishing.com/trees.

Previously published as part of a larger volume, *The Illustrated World Encyclopedia of Saints*

PUBLISHER'S NOTE

Although the advice and information in this book are believed to be accurate and true at the time of going to press, neither the authors nor the publisher can accept any legal responsibility or liability for any errors or omissions that may have been made.

PICTURE CREDITS

The publishers would like to thank the following agencies for permission to use their images:
akg-images 7b, 9t, 10t, 17, 19, 13b, 21tl, tr and b, 22t, 25t, 26t and b, 27, 28b, 29t, 30b, 32b, 38t, 41t and b, 42b, 45b and tl,47m, 53bm, 54l, 55l, 56l, 57tr, 44r, 57b, 64t, 65br, 72b, 73t, 81b, 82t, 83b, 86l, 89, 68t, 69, 74l, 93b, 44m, 47t, 49br, 51tr, 52b, 57tl, 62t;
Alamy 60b;
ArkReligion.com 63tl, tr and b;
The Art Archive/Gianni Dagli Orti 15, 28t, 29bl, 61t, 67t and b, 84bl and t;
The Bridgeman Art Library 10b, 11r, 13t,14b and tl, 16t, 22b, 24t, 25br, 29br, 31b, 34b, 37r, 39br, 49tr, 51b, 54b, 58t and b, 60t and m, 66bl, 63b, 76b, 78t;
Corbis 6b, 8, 12b, 14tr,16b, 23, 31t, 32t, 33t, br, and bl, 34t, 35, 36, 43b, 45tr, 46tl and tr, 48t and b, 53br, 55r, 59bl, 62m, 76t, 77t, 78b, 79b, 89b, 87b, 92t; **Getty** 24b, 30t, 62b, 25bl, 7t, 18b, 87t, 49tl, 53bl, 52t, 73b, 53t, 43t, 88b;
Sonia Halliday Photographs 6t, 18t, 20t and b, 38b, 39t and bl, 40t and b, 47b, 49bl, 56r, 59t, 79t.

CONTENTS

Introduction	6	Patron Saints of Professions	44	Mark	77
		Religious Orders	46	Luke	78
SAINTHOOD	8	Patron Saints of Nations	48	Stephen	79
Saints in the Early Church	10	Fourteen Holy Helpers	50	Eustace	79
Doctors of the Church	12	Warrior Saints	52	James the Great	80
Eastern Saints	14	The Saints in Art	54	Peter	81
Canonization	16	Royal Saints	56	Andrew	82
Mysteries and Miracles	18	Saintly Popes	58	Paul	83
Holy Relics	20	The Martyrs of China	60	Cecelia	84
Medieval Pilgrimage	22	Incorruptibles	62	George	85
Important Feast Days	24	Houses of God	64	Christopher	86
Heroes and Martyrs	26	The Cult of Mary	66	Jerome	87
New Worlds	28	Patron Saints	68	Benedict	88
Modern Pilgrims	30			Francis of Assisi	89
The Blessed	32			Joan of Arc	90
All Saints and All Souls	34	**VENERATED**		Ignatius of Loyola	91
		SAINTS	70	Theresa of Ávila	92
		Mary the Virgin	72	Bernadette of Lourdes	93
THE ROLES		John the Baptist	73	Theresa of Liseux	94
OF SAINTS	36	Mary Magdalene	74		
The Holy Family	38	Thomas	75		
The Apostles	40	Matthew	76	Index	95
Child Saints	42	John	76		

INTRODUCTION

A SAINT IS A DECEASED INDIVIDUAL WHOSE EXCEPTIONAL HOLINESS CHRISTIANS BELIEVE HAS EARNED HIM OR HER A PLACE IN HEAVEN. THERE, SAINTS ACT AS CELESTIAL AGENTS. THE FAITHFUL MAY PRAY TO THEM AND BESEECH THEM TO CONVEY THEIR PRAYERS TO GOD.

Above Detail from the Communion of the Apostles, *a 15th-century fresco at Platanistasa in the Nicosia District of Cyprus.*

Saints are not gods; they are not worshipped. But they are believed to exist so close to God in heaven that they fulfil a key role as intermediaries for the Roman Catholic and Eastern Orthodox Churches.

WHAT IS A SAINT?

From the earliest days of the Church, the cultus of veneration developed to include figures besides Jesus who were deemed to be holy. Their lives, which showed great piety and humility, served as inspiration to the inchoate community of believers.

On the day of their death, these holy individuals were believed to have been reborn into God's presence. Possessing this elevated status, the saints quickly developed cult followings. Their death was commemorated with a feast day at which time typically the faithful would gather at the saint's tomb. The bodily remains, or relics, were believed to possess power. Not only were saints in a privileged position to get prayers answered, they could also work fabulous miracles.

MARTYRS

The judgement of an individual's imitation of Christ in this early period of Christianity was concerned as much with the manner of their death as with the conduct of their life. A martyr –

he who dies for the Christian faith – became an automatic choice for the company of saints. As the Church grew, especially once the pope became the sole authority in conferring such status in the 2nd millennium, other factors became as important, if not more so, in determining the qualites of a saint.

HEROIC VIRTUE

Those who did not die a martyr had to be shown by their cultus to have led a life of "heroic virtue", as it is defined by the Vatican. In Christian terms, this means they must have abandoned worldly interests. Whatever their station in life, whether prince or pauper, their devotion to faith in Jesus had to be manifest in their humility, charity and prayer.

As bureaucracy and suspicion played ever greater roles in the assessment process, so fewer saints were created. The late John Paul II did much to rationalize and clarify the procedure of canonization (literally, adding a name to the canon of saints).

Right From the early Renaissance, Madonna Enthroned with Saints *(Domenico Ghirlandaio, 1484).*

ABOUT THIS BOOK

The study of saints is fraught with difficulty; many saints have been forgotten over time, while thousands of names are obscure or entirely absent from historical record. This book gives an explanation of sainthood, defining its role and purpose within the Church. It then details the ways saints have been important during the centuries of human and religious history, and finishes with a chapter that celebrates the 25 most venerated saints, including, among others, Mary the Virgin, the Apostles, St George, St Francis, and St Theresa of Avila.

The book shows that while all Christian saints ae identical in their devotion to God, each one has their own talent and personality, and their own story of struggle. It also shows that human affinity to sainthood is similarly diverse, and that our response to the history and characters of these holy people is as rich and complex as the personalities of the saints themselves.

Right A panel showing Christ and the apostles at Pentecost (Georgian School, 12th century).

SAINTS IN OTHER FAITHS

Veneration of holy people, as messengers of the Almighty, has a place outside the Christian faith, too. Judaism refers to a category of holy figures known as Tzadikkim. In Islam, certain holy men, known as *Sufis*, are remembered with festivals. Thousands of Muslims in Pakistan, for example, commemorate the life and death of a 12th-century Sufi, Lal Shahbaz Qalandar, with sacred songs and dances performed by dervishes (followers of Sufism).

In Hinduism, *Sadhus*, or holy men, are considered to have reached saintly status while still alive. Likewise in Buddhism, *Arhats* are monks who are considered to have reached a state of nirvana.

Although there are some similarities in concept between the faiths, each has its own meaning. None is identical with that of Christian sainthood, which constitutes a unique doctrine of heavenly community.

Right Dancing dervishes from a Persian miniature (c.1650).

SAINTHOOD

The company of saints is filled with souls from all walks of life. These former human beings have been granted the highest accolade that their fellow Christians can give in honour of their holiness and worldly achievements.

In this section, Sainthood, there is a clear explanation of the qualities a person must show before they are officially recognized as a saint. Many have devoted their lives to spreading the word of God; others have sacrificed their own well-being for the welfare of their fellow men, women and children. Believers choose candidates for sainthood from a spontaneous understanding of their superior qualities as humans, but the Church is more circumspect in granting this status.

Official and non-official attitudes within the Church are given a full history, and the religious beliefs surrounding saints are clearly described. Also covered is the alteration of custom and religious practice brought by the religious wars of the Reformation, a change that affected the regard in which saints are now held. Ritual expressions of faith, such as pilgrimages and the veneration of shrines and relics, are analysed in both historic and modern expressions. Feast days and the festivals that have developed around these occasions are discussed. The reasoning behind certain saints being selected as patrons of nations, professions and causes is explained. This is not a history of the Church, but a revelation of the role saints play in art and the prayers of the faithful.

Left Detail of Procession in St Mark's Square *(Gentile Bellini, c.1500).*

Top Twelfth Night Altarpiece *on wood. St Ursula and companions (left), the Adoration of the Kings (middle) and St Gereon with companions (right) (Stefan Lochner, c.1440).*

SAINTS IN THE EARLY CHURCH

THE FIRST CHRISTIANS WERE FORBIDDEN TO PRACTISE THEIR FAITH AND WERE CRUELLY PERSECUTED BY THE ROMANS. MANY EVEN DIED FOR THEIR BELIEFS. THESE MARTYRS WERE HONOURED AS SAINTS BY THEIR FELLOW BELIEVERS IN THE EARLY CHURCH.

There has never been any argument over the saintly status of the Holy Family, or the apostles and friends of Jesus on earth, but other saints have had slower recognition, or their status has been disputed. The earliest figures chosen for sainthood were usually those who died as martyrs.

Christianity was born in Palestine, a land that was then part of the Roman Empire. The Roman authorities who had condemned Jesus to death forbade any practice of his faith. Periodic state persecutions of Christians were merciless.

Whole communities who refused to abandon their faith were massacred, and some individuals suffered hideous torture. Some, dressed in rags with no weapon, were pitted against well-armed Roman gladiators, or fierce beasts. Thousands were murdered. While the names of many survive, we know few details beyond the date, and perhaps the place, of their death.

Records of these martyrs, the first Christians, can be read in the grave inscriptions found in the catacombs of Rome where the dead were laid to rest.

EARLIEST MARTYRS

The first martyr (protomartyr) known to us was murdered about five years after the death of Christ. St Stephen was carried to the outskirts of Jerusalem and stoned to death. As he fell to his knees, he cried out, "Lord, lay not this sin to their charge." Thus, in his dying, he showed his belief in

Below The martyrdom of St Erasmus as illustrated in the Golden Legend, *a 13th-century hagiography of saints written by Jacobus de Voragine.*

Above St Agnes, fellow virgins and singing angels in an altarpiece from the Upper Rhine (c.1460).

Jesus' message of love and forgiveness towards the wrongdoer. Many of the early martyrs showed a similar courage in their deaths. St Catherine of Alexandria endured the cruel spikes of a wheel. St Lucy refused to forsake her faith, even under torture, and was savagely beheaded.

It must be accepted that many legends grew up around the martyrs. For instance, although Lucy's tormentors had gouged out her eyes, it was said that she could fit them back into their sockets. Likewise, it was said that divine intervention broke Catherine's wheel, rescuing her from pain. Sebastian survived being tied to a column and shot through by a shower of arrows. And when Januarius was thrown to the lions, the beasts refused to attack him, instead laying quiescent at his feet. There are accounts of saints being thrown into vats of boiling oil and

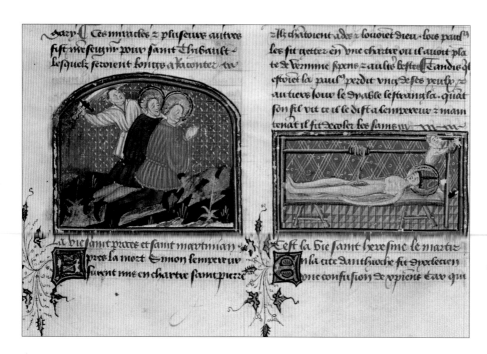

emerging unscathed. Others who suffered a beheading were said to have merely replaced their heads.

BLESSED VIRGINS

Many of the earliest female saints were chosen not only for their status as martyrs, but also for their purity in imitation of the Blessed Virgin. The importance of virginity has always been a strong (but not essential) consideration in the sainthood of women. As late as the 15th century, when St Joan of Arc claimed this status, she was given humiliating physical inspections to test the truth of her words.

During the Roman persecutions, St Agnes, at the age of 14, consecrated her virginity to Christ. She refused marriage, and both her faith and innocence were put to the sword. St Irene, a young girl, was forced by the Romans to go naked into a brothel, but she radiated such purity that no man dared go near her. She was martyred in AD 305. In the same century the most extravagant legend of proud virgins involves the British St Ursula and her 11,000 virgin companions. Forced to flee their homelands to avoid "violation" through marriage, they finally reached Germany. There they were martyred for their beliefs, yet they died joyously.

TRUTH IN LEGEND

Sceptics tend to dismiss these tales. But Christians honour them because they symbolize the superhuman courage and piety of the persecuted, and confirm that all suffering is eased by faith in Christ. As the novelist Sir Arthur Conan Doyle once said, "a legend however exaggerated upon fact is its own fact, witnessing belief." Although in many cases these stories are embellishments of a terrible reality, they still hold a certain truth for believers.

CATACOMBS OF ROME

Beneath the city of Rome lies a great labyrinth of caves and tunnels. Probably first used by pagans as burial grounds, the early Christians tunnelled into this underground world to lay their dead. Some of the catacombs had been dug out to form large halls with connecting chapels. Recesses were hollowed out to hold three or four bodies apiece. They were sealed with slabs of marble or tiles bearing inscriptions and motifs. The labyrinth was also used as a place of refuge to escape Roman persecutors. By the late 4th century AD, the catacombs were no longer burial vaults but pilgrimage sites, which are still visited today.

Above The interior of a catacomb in Rome dating from the 3rd century AD.

Left One of the 40 martyrs of Sebaste being killed in AD 320, during the Roman persecution of Christians under the rule of Emperor Licinius (Byzantine, 12th century).

DOCTORS OF THE CHURCH

LEADERS EMERGED FROM THE EARLY CHRISTIAN COMMUNITIES TO HELP DEVELOP THE STRUCTURE OF THE CHURCH. LEARNED WRITERS AND THINKERS AMONG THEM WHO MADE SIGNIFICANT CONTRIBUTIONS WERE CALLED "DOCTORS OF THE CHURCH".

A landmark change in the fortunes of the Church occurred early in the 4th century AD when Emperor Constantine I converted to Christianity. His edict permitting the worship of all faiths meant saints were no longer chosen primarily for their martyrdom. More important was the purity of a life dedicated to Christ. Some did so by renouncing the world, others played key roles in developing the Church for the benefit of the flock.

Scholarly writers and thinkers worked on formulating doctrine for the Church. Some helped develop new forms of prayer and

Above St Augustine of Hippo *(Piero della Francesca, 15th century).*

ritual. The greatest among these learned Christians were the early "Doctors of the Church", a term meaning great teachers. Unlike other saints who are championed by the people, the Church authorities alone decide who is worthy to receive this title.

GREAT TEACHERS

To be recognized as a Doctor, the saint must formulate a special doctrine. Alternatively, he or she may make a profound interpretation of the faith, as well as having a "remarkable holiness" of life.

St Jerome (c.AD 341–420), who started his life as a monk, translated the Bible from Greek into Latin. St Ambrose interpreted the significance of the sacraments, and

Left Detail of St Ambrose from the fresco Doctors of the Church *(Giotto di Bondone, 13th century).*

defended the authority vested in the office of the pope. St Gregory the Great (*c*.AD 540–604) was a successful missionary, notably directing the conversion of the English. St Augustine of Hippo's interpretation of Christ's message profoundly influenced Christian moral principles.

MODERN DECLARATIONS

Recognition as a Doctor of the Church could be a long process, sometimes taking centuries to complete. Sts Ambrose, Jerome, Augustine of Hippo and Gregory the Great all lived before the 8th century, but they were not declared Doctors until Pope Benedict XIV came to office in 1740.

The tradition of creating doctorships still continues today. St Theresa of Lisieux (1873–97) was declared a Doctor by John Paul II in 1997 for her simple but inspirational devotion. She is now one of the most popular of saints.

Above St Gregory in the Golden Legend *(Jacobus de Voragine, c.1370).*

DESERT FATHERS

Christ said, "If any man will follow me, let him deny himself, take up his cross and follow me" (Mark 8:34). In the first centuries of Christianity, there were believers who took these words as a direction to forsake all earthly pleasure. They followed the example of John the Baptist in hoping that hardship would wash away their sinful selves, and isolated themselves from society by living in deserts and other uninhabited places.

They led harsh lives, with little food. Legends say they were fed by ravens or wolves, and that water gushed from stony wastelands. The genuine humility and devotion shown by these ascetics attracted others, and soon groups of hermits chose to inhabit huts and caves close to each other.

From these loose communities, particularly those in Egypt, emerged teachers known as the "Desert Fathers". First among them was St Pachomius who lived alone on the banks of the Nile until other ascetics gathered around him. Some were so fanatical in their contempt for their own bodies they risked starvation and madness. To impose some constraints, Pachomius set up a community of 100 followers who committed to abide by his "Rules". To vows of chastity, poverty and obedience, he added orders of prayer and routine.

By his death, *c*.AD 346, Pachomius had founded ten monasteries, among the first such Christian institutions. Another popular Egyptian hermit of the 4th century, St Antony, also organized a monastic community. Over the centuries many other founders have established similar orders.

Above This 12th-century wall painting from Macedonia depicts St Antony, sometimes referred to as "the eremite" for his desert life.

EASTERN SAINTS

THE CHURCHES OF RUSSIA, EASTERN EUROPE AND THE MIDDLE EAST DEVELOPED THEIR OWN THEOLOGY, VARYING FROM THAT OF ROMAN CATHOLICISM. EASTERN SAINTS FORM A DISTINCT COMPANY AND EVOKE A PARTICULAR KIND OF VENERATION.

The Eastern Church treats its saints in a slightly different way from that of Rome. Saints are not approached primarily as a means of conveying prayers to God, but rather to bring the believer closer to the reality of God. The reason for this difference lies in the Eastern Church's separate development in history from the West.

A formal schism between Western and Eastern Christians in 1054 led to the formation of a branch of Christendom known as the Eastern Orthodox Church. The two branches of Christianity had different beliefs about the dual nature of Christ, as both man and God.

The Roman Catholic and Orthodox Churches both believe that Christ is the Son of God who nevertheless assumed human form. The Orthodox interprets this to mean humans can attain the spiritual

Left An icon of St Gregory Palamas (Russian School, 19th century).

Above Mosaic detail in the apse of the Basilica Eufrasiana in Porec, Croatia (4th century). The work draws the eye to focus on the Blessed Virgin and the Christ child.

qualities of God; the Roman Church believes humans can only strive for these qualities.

The Orthodox Church has not altered its dogma or ritual since the 8th century. So tradition is paramount, and the saints form a key part of their worship.

EARLY HOLY FIGURES

Pre-eminent among the Eastern saints is the Blessed Virgin. But everyone who is in heaven is a saint for the Orthodox, including pre-Christian Jews such as Moses. Popular early saints, such as John, Nicholas of Myra, George and Christopher, are common to both branches, but post-medieval saints are not.

The Orthodox categorize their saints according to type: prophets (those who foretold the coming of

Left Detail from a manuscript showing St Sergius of Radonezh overseeing the building of a church (Andrei Rublev, 15th century).

Jesus), the apostles, martyrs, Church Doctors (or Fathers), monastics (Desert Fathers) and the just (those who imitate Christ).

St John Chrysostom is highly honoured as a preacher and teacher. In AD 398, he was elected as archbishop of Constantinople (now Istanbul) and is recognized as a Doctor of the Church.

Another Doctor is St Basil the Great (c.AD 330–79) who laid down rules of organization for monastic life. His friend, St Gregory of Nazianzus, also ranks high among Orthodox saints.

BYZANTINE MYSTICS

St Gregory's spiritual theology was developed by Simeon the New Theologian (d.1022) to reach a high point in Byzantine mysticism. Another Gregory, of

Below The transfiguration of Christ in an Armenian manuscript (1362).

Sinai (d.1346), devised new methods of meditation that influenced Orthodox practice. Other saints include Sergius of Radonezh (c.1315–92), monastic founder beloved of the Russians.

Mount Athos in Greece has a tradition of saintliness. Here the monk St Gregory Palamas (d.1359) founded an ascetical order, Hesychasm. Controversially it claimed visions of God's "uncreated light", an idea later accepted.

WINDOWS INTO HEAVEN

The Eastern Orthodox Church regards images of the holy saints as "windows of perception". It is believed these images open a vista leading to God. By so doing, they convey the message of the gospels.

Images of saints often appear on icons and architectural mosaics, rarely as statues. Depictions are lavishly decorated, with details worked in gold. In following the traditional Byzantine style of art, these images reflect the conservative nature of the Orthodox Church.

The icons are portable, being painted on three folding panels, and are designed as objects of meditation. By creating "a window into heaven", their contemplation and prayer increases the spirituality of the believer, bringing them closer to a knowledge of God.

Whether in church or at home, the icon is positioned with reverence. It may be surrounded by candles or placed near a crucifix, creating the appearance of a small altar. But the icon is never an object of worship. It is a symbol and an aid to spiritual awareness.

CANONIZATION

As the Church grew, its communities revered more and more devout figures as saints. The need to control the creation of sainthood resulted in the establishment of a system of universal recognition in a canon of holy souls.

Although some living people are described as saints, to be a real saint, the person must be dead. Up until the 4th century AD, when Christianity was adopted as the official religion of the Roman Empire, the devout were made saints only if they had died for their faith, for example were martyrs.

In the early, unstructured Church, groups began to identify individuals who, in their life and particularly in their death, imitated Christ. Such a group, known even today as a "cult" or "cultus", acknowledged the saintly qualities of the individual at their death.

The cultus prepared a joyous burial at which the death was celebrated with the eucharist. The

Below Pope John Paul II canonized 120 Chinese martyrs in a ceremony held in St Peter's Square, Rome, on 1 October 2000.

earthly remains, or relics, of the saint were carefully wrapped in an effort to preserve them. Every anniversary of the death called for a reunion of followers, and this day came to be known as the saint's "feast day".

GROWTH OF CULTUSES

The proclamation of these devout members of local communities as saints was based on no established criteria in the early period. Vague ideas of holiness based on manner of life and death were frequently supported by claims of miracles and visions.

By the 4th century AD, local priests or bishops were being drawn into debate on the worthiness of these decisions. In some cases, for instance, there was suspicion that a person had committed suicide in the hope of being granted the glory of a martyr-

Above Pope Pius II canonizes St Catherine of Siena *(Pinturicchio, 16th century).*

saint. This was a particular problem among the desert hermits of North Africa. So priests began to assess the claims of the cultuses.

Bishops saw formal procedures of investigation as the best way to tackle the growth of false cultuses. Priests kept records of saints and the reasons for their sanctification.

PAPAL SAINTS ONLY

At last, in the 12th century, the right to confer, or "canonize", sainthood was reserved for the Holy See, the office of the pope.

The official implementation of this development was attributed to Pope Alexander III (1159–81), though recent scholarship prefers Innocent III (1199–1216). From the 13th century, papal commissions were ordered to investigate claims to sainthood. The cultuses continued to select an individual but the commission required evidence that the candidate had lived a life worthy of Christ. Any claims

to miracles were to be thoroughly investigated by the Church. These rules are followed to this day, although in 1983 Pope John Paul II streamlined the regulations, making them more precise.

MAKING A SAINT

Step One: The cultus makes its choice of saint, but the local bishop does not automatically accept it. For five years after the candidate's death, he conducts research into his or her virtues, or the circumstances of martyrdom. This allows time for a calm assessment of the candidate's life and death.

Then, the bishop's approval is submitted to the Congregation for the Causes of Saints, a panel made up of theologians and cardinals of the Church. If the panel

DECANONIZATION

The Holy See knows the early saints have poor records, if any, to support their status. But it generally accepts the situation.

However, the Holy See did decanonize St Barbara in 1969 and Simon of Trent in 1965 because they were purely legendary characters. St Brigid of Ireland was accused of being a pagan figure, and so she too was decanonized.

Official announcements are often ignored. Cultuses can remain attached to saints, despite formal abolishment. In recognition of this loyalty, the Church has allowed certain cultuses to venerate "their" saint, but has withdrawn universal recognition.

Some decanonized saints in history include: Barbara, Brigid of Ireland, Christopher, George, Philomena, Simon of Trent, Valentine and William of Norwich.

approves, the name is submitted to the pope who then declares the candidate "Venerable".

Step Two: Martyrs will be canonized by the pope, but the Venerable must now be supported by a written claim from the recipient of a purported miracle performed by the holy candidate.

This miracle must occur after the death of the candidate. The believer must avow that they prayed to the Venerable who then interceded with God in answer to that prayer. This is seen as proof that the dead one's spirit is close to God. The pope approves the beatification of the candidate, who

Above Detail from a fresco showing the canonization of St Francis by Pope Gregory IX (Giotto di Bondone, c.1295).

can now be venerated by his or her cultus as "Blessed". Mother Teresa of Calcutta is an example.

Step Three: The third and last step towards sainthood needs evidence of one more miracle. When the pope has this, he agrees to canonize the beatified who is then named a saint. This status identifies the person as one who lived and died in imitation of Christ, and is officially in heaven. He or she can be honoured by all.

MYSTERIES AND MIRACLES

LEGENDS OF MIRACLES AND EXTRAORDINARY BRAVERY ARE WELL-KNOWN ATTRIBUTES OF THE SAINTS, BUT SOME WERE WITNESSED MANIFESTING MYSTERIOUS POWERS AND PHYSICAL CHANGES THAT DEFY SCIENTIFIC EXPLANATION.

Saints were so named because they led lives in imitation of Christ. It followed therefore that, like Jesus, they might be capable of performing miracles. The early saints were credited with having all sorts of supernatural powers. Evil spirits, disease, mortal enemies and wild animals were all claimed to be overcome. The perceived holiness of saints and their closeness to God led the faithful to believe that their prayers might be answered, and in miraculous fashion, too. Once a devout Christian had been declared a

Above St Denys is said to have carried his severed head to his burial place, as shown in this stained glass window in St Aignan Church, Chartres, France.

saint, their lives often became embellished with events of the miraculous, such as inexplicable cures or angelic assistance.

VOICES AND VISIONS
St Joan of Arc claimed she had heard the voices of three saints instructing her to save France. The mystic and writer St Hildegard of Bingen described heavenly visions she experienced during her life. Crowds of people in Milan heard a unearthly child's voice calling out repeatedly, "Ambrose for bishop." The divine message persuaded them to elect Ambrose, despite him being unbaptized.

Another account of a divine apparition involved St Isidore the farmer, a humble, browbeaten peasant. He was so tired and in

Left St Januarius visited in prison by Proculus and Sosius (Francesco Solimena, c.1700).

such pain from beatings he could not work, but two angels appeared and ploughed the fields for him.

St Clement was said to have experienced a vision of Jesus while suffering extreme thirst digging a quarry under Roman coercion. The vision which came in answer to the saint's prayers was accompanied by a spring of water gushing suddenly from the rocks.

HEALING

The more obvious imitation of Christ involves miraculous cures reminiscent of his ministry, such as healing disease. St Odile, for example, was said to have been born blind, but was given sight after her baptism. During her life, she restored the sight of others.

Saints' relics were believed to have the power to effect miraculous cures. Pilgrims travelled great distances to be in the presence of a saint's tomb, so that they might receive the healing power believed to reside within the corpse.

The relics of St Martin, for instance, were said to ooze curative oil and the faithful would flock to his tomb for a mere dab. Likewise, in the 7th century, oil was said to weep from the tomb of St John the Baptist and bore the odour of the honey upon which he had survived.

RESCUE

Miraculous cures save the body from physical peril. Closely associated in terms of salvation are the rescues of individuals or whole communities from evil, frequently in the shape of a human enemy.

A painting of Our Lady of Czestochowa, commonly referred to as the Black Madonna, became the focus of Polish nationalism in the 14th century. When the Hussites overran the monastery of Jasna Gora (Mount of Light) in 1430, the painting was said to resist all attempts to destroy it. Every subsequent siege failed and Our Lady of Czestochowa was officially named Queen of Poland.

In times of war, saints are invoked for their protection, especially in great peril. And when victory comes against all odds, guardian angels and patron saints often receive the credit.

The blood of St Januarius has been revered in Naples ever since 1631 when Mt Vesuvius erupted. Subsequent prayers to the saint are believed to have prevented any repetition of such a disaster. Every year the vial containing the blood is displayed. If it liquefies the year will be free from disaster.

THE STIGMATA

The appearance of wounds on the hands, feet and in the ribs, in imitation of those made by the nails that pinned Christ to the Cross, are a phenomenon known as the stigmata. St Francis of Assisi was the first Christian to manifest the marks, in 1224, which remained on his body for two years until his death. Since then, the Catholic Church has recognized 62 men and women as stigmatics. Listed below are the best-known sufferers, some saints, others Blessed.

St Angela of Foligno
Blessed Baptista Varani
Blessed Carlo of Sezze
St Catherine of Genoa
Blessed Catherine of
  Racconigi
St Catherine de' Ricci
St Catherine of Siena
St Clare of Montefalco
St Colette
St Francis of Assisi
St Frances of Rome
St Gertrude
St John of God
St Lidwina
Blessed Lucy of Narnia
St Lutgardis

St Margaret of Cortona
Blessed Margaret Mary
  Alacoque
Blessed Marie de l'Incarnation
Blessed Mary Anne of Jesus
St Mary Frances of the Five
  Wounds
St Mary Magdalene de' Pazzi
Blessed Osanna of Mantua
Padre Pio (*St Pius of Pietrelcina*)
St Rita of Cascia
St Veronica Giuliani

Right St Francis of Assisi receiving the stigmata on the mountain of La Verna in Italy (School of Bonaventura Berlinghieri, 13th century).

HOLY RELICS

WHETHER SKELETON OR MERE SCRAP OF CLOTHING, RELICS WERE BELIEVED TO REPRESENT A SAINT'S PRESENCE ON EARTH. FOR THE DEVOUT, THEIR POWER WAS SUCH THAT EVEN SIGHT OF THESE ARTEFACTS WAS SAID TO EFFECT MIRACULOUS CURES.

From the earliest period of Christianity, the bodily remains of saints were venerated. A custom developed in which the saint's relics were no longer buried or laid in catacombs, but placed beneath church altars.

Churches sheltering relics were perceived by St Augustine of Hippo to be "as tombs of mortal men, whose spirits live with God". To this day, in the Roman Catholic Church, altars upon which mass is celebrated must contain the relics of a saint, according to canon law.

Gradually, the term "relic" embraced lengths of bone, scraps of burial wrappings, jewellery. Indeed, it could mean any little thing that had once belonged to the saint. The Church accepted this development because in the 1st century AD in Ephesus, Turkey, tradition held that God had performed miracles through the handkerchiefs and aprons of St Paul. The sick believed they had been cured simply through their proximity to Paul's clothing.

The faithful believed that their prayers for forgiveness were more likely to be heard when uttered before relics or tombs. Other believers claimed the very sight of the relic summoned forth the saint who, through God, might perform miraculous cures of any ailment, from warts to infertility.

COLLECTORS' ITEMS

Holy sites were not limited to the saints' burial places but included any site where a relic was housed. Their bodily relics became valuable, some fetching large sums, and were often plundered

Above A reliquary of the hand of St Thomas Becket kept at Burgos Cathedral, Spain.

THE HOLY HOUSE

The story attached to the "Holy House" of Loreto in Italy indicates the crazed, but profound, attachment medieval Christians had for their greatest saints.

According to the extravagant legend, an angel lifted the house in Nazareth where Joseph and the Virgin Mary had once lived, and carried it away. The house landed in random places before finally coming to rest in Loreto. The event was precisely recorded as ending on 7 September 1295. So many pilgrims flocked to see this wondrous relic, coined the "Holy House", that the authorities constructed an imposing church on the site. It continues to attract visitors.

Right The Basilica (Holy House) of Loreto, Italy, is one of the most revered sites in the Christian world. It was built in 1469 to house what is believed to be the miraculously transported home of the Virgin Mary.

by clergy and believers who strove to build up collections. In the process relics were moved – "translated" – from one place to another. There could be a finger at one church, a shinbone elsewhere, while a third might claim to have a saint's sandal or cloak.

The faithful might ideally have wished to visit tombs, but a relic would serve just as well. It held the power of the saint. Even the churches of Jerusalem, whose significance rested on their association with the sites of Jesus' passion, boasted ownership of the relics of the True Cross upon which the Saviour had suffered crucifixion.

Every Christian pilgrim longed to visit the shrine of a saint, and many collected relics. The more precious items were kept in beautiful caskets, known as reliquaries, shaped like small tombs.

These containers were wrought in precious metals and adorned with jewels and enamelled images. Many are treasured to this day in Roman Catholic and Eastern Orthodox churches, although most are housed in museums across Europe and the USA.

STRANGE AND BIZARRE
Some of the more interesting relics include a small carving of St Foy (also known as St Faith), from the 9th century. The figure is covered in gold plate and, over the centuries, believers bedecked the surface with precious emeralds, pearls and amethysts. This martyr was just 12 years old when she died. In the back of the carving there is a cavity containing her tiny wrapped skull.

Pope Urban V had the head of St Cassian encased in an elaborate casket. But Charlemagne (Charles the Great AD 747–814), emperor of the Holy Roman Empire, did better than that. He built a cathedral to house his huge collection of relics.

Among them, he claimed, were the cloth that once wrapped the decapitated head of John the Baptist, the tunic of the Virgin Mary, and swaddling cloths of the Infant Jesus. His collection of relics was displayed every seven years for a week in July. Vast crowds visited the church in Aachen, formerly Aix-la-Chapelle. The custom is still followed, revealing 200 relics every seventh year.

Right A reliquary of St Foy (also known as St Faith) made of gold and jewels, held in the church in Conques, France (9th century).

Above left This reliquary depicts the martyrdom of the Roman St Candidus. It is made of nutwood and covered in gold and silver (c.1165).

Above Reliquary of St Stephen with enamel work from Limoges (12th century).

MEDIEVAL PILGRIMAGE

A JOURNEY TO VISIT THE SACRED RELICS OF A SAINT WAS AN IMPORTANT ACT OF DEVOTION IN THE MIDDLE AGES. THE HEALING POWER BELIEVED TO RESIDE IN THEM, AND THE SPIRITUAL ENERGY ASSOCIATED WITH THEIR SHRINES, DREW HORDES OF PILGRIMS.

Early Christians believed it an important act of piety to pray at the places where the Saviour and his company of saints had lived and died. A pilgrimage involved hardship. It was a form of penance, a humble mission to offer prayers of contrition, and call on the saints to intercede with God. From as early as the 2nd century AD, records tell of Christians travelling great distances on foot to the Holy Land in order to visit Bethlehem and Jerusalem.

They would have had a hard job, for these sites in Palestine were lost after AD 132, when the Roman emperor Hadrian demolished Jerusalem and rebuilt the city with temples dedicated to Roman gods. Only in AD 326, when Emperor Constantine I ordered Christian bishops to find the sites of Christ's passion, were shrines and churches built there.

One such site, the Holy Sepulchre, built by Constantine himself, stands to this day, albeit with some modification. The emperor's mother, St Helen, also a convert, founded churches in the Holy Land which drew yet more pilgrims.

HEART OF THE EMPIRE

Outside the Holy Land, the most significant destination was Rome. Here the tombs and relics of the Holy Martyrs, including Sts Peter and Paul, were located. In AD 326,

Above The chapel at Aachen Minster was built AD 788–805 for Emperor Charlemagne to house his huge collection of relics.

St Helen brought to the city a marble staircase taken from the judgement hall of Pontius Pilate in Jerusalem. Purported to be the very steps upon which Christ had trodden as he went to his trial, these Holy Stairs were installed in the church of St John Lateran, and are said to be stained with Christ's blood. To this day, pilgrims climb the 28 stairs on their knees.

ROADS THROUGH EUROPE

In England, thousands trekked to Canterbury to see the relics of St Thomas Becket, or made their way to Norfolk to pray before the holy shrine of Our Lady of Walsingham. Pilgrims took the Via Francigena, a popular route from Canterbury to Rome.

On the way was Paris, with Christ's crown of thorns, and Chartres, which held the holy tunic of the Virgin Mary. Pilgrims

Left An illustration from John Lydgate's The Troy Book and The Siege of Thebes, *shows pilgrims leaving Canterbury for London (1412–22).*

flocked to Tours, where the relics of St Martin were kept. And Cologne, in Germany, possessed the relics of the Magi, the three wise men who visited the stable to pay homage to the baby Jesus.

Once in Italy, pilgrims could glimpse the Holy Shroud of Jesus in Turin. And travelling on southwards, they would throng the streets of Assisi where St Francis was buried. From all over Europe, devout Christians journeyed to Santiago de Compostela in Spain, where the relics of St James the Great lay in his tomb.

IMPACT OF REFORM

Pilgrimage had become so popular, even hysterical in its folksy enthusiam, that the whole activity invited disdain in some quarters. The bishop of Salisbury was moved to describe the veneration of relics as "abominable idolatry".

In 1517, the German priest Martin Luther introduced a radical idea. He argued Christians

NEW MARTYR SAINTS

A major consequence of the Reformation (1517–1648) was that new martyrs joined the company of saints. Hundreds of Welsh and English Roman Catholics were burnt, crushed between milling stones or beheaded by Protestants during the religious strife.

Some deaths were political in intent, and since then 200 have been named as martyrs. In 1970, Pope Paul VI found 40 to be worthy of canonization. They are known as the Forty Martyrs of England and Wales. Of these, 13 were priests, 20 monks and friars, and the remaining 7 consisted of lay men and women.

Above The Church of the Holy Sepulchre in Jerusalem, c.AD 335, commemorates the tomb of Christ and is a special place of pilgrimage.

could approach God for forgiveness, without the intercession of the saints. So began the great division in the Church, the Reformation, which separated Christians into Roman Catholics and Protestants.

As Christendom became a battlefield, shrines were destroyed and relics burnt. In England, the shrine of St Thomas Becket was melted down to enrich the king's coffers, and the beautiful shrine in Walsingham violated.

Even Luther, the angry reformer, was distressed at such destruction wrought by the mobs. After these calamitous events, relics no longer gripped the religious mind. Pilgrimages, too, lost their worldly appeal and were not the major social events they were in the pre-Reformation period.

Instead, pilgrimages reverted to being the pious causes of penance they had once been. Modern believers still honour relics, even venerate them, especially on feast days. Some recently canonized saints, such as the Aztec peasant Juan Diego, command huge followings of pilgrims who come to witness their relics.

IMPORTANT FEAST DAYS

FEAST DAYS, TRADITIONALLY SET TO MARK THE DAY OF THE SAINT'S DEATH, ARE A CELEBRATION OF BIRTH INTO HEAVEN. CHURCHES CONDUCT SPECIAL MASSES, AS WELL AS PUBLIC EVENTS OUTDOORS. PROCESSIONS, MUSIC AND DANCE INVOLVE THE WHOLE COMMUNITY.

Roman Catholics and members of the Orthodox Churches venerate the saints' feast days in their liturgy. Important saints are celebrated on these days with special processions, particularly when the church houses their relics and images.

Above Thomas Aquinas being received into the Dominican order *(German School, 16th century). His feast day is 28 January.*

JANUARY
Gregory of Nazianzus, Basil the
 Great 2
Genevieve 3
Elizabeth Seton 4
Sava 14
Antony of Egypt 17
Sebastian 20
John the Almsgiver 23
Thomas Aquinas 28

FEBRUARY
Brigid of Ireland 1
Agatha 5

Below Russian priests celebrating the feast day of St Cyril and St Methodius, known as "apostles to the Slavs", in 2007.

Jerome Emiliani 8
Valentine, Cyril and
 Methodius 14
Martyrs of China 17

MARCH
David of Wales, Gregory of
 Nyssa 1
Katharine Drexel 3
Patrick, Joseph of Arimathea 17
Joseph (husband of Mary) 19
Cuthbert 20

APRIL
Isidore of Seville 4
John-Baptist de La Salle 7
Teresa of Los Andes 12
Bernadette of Lourdes 16
Anselm 21
George 23
Mark 25
Catherine of Siena 29

MAY
John 6
Pachomius (West) 9
Helen with Constantine (East) 21
Rita of Cascia 22

Madeleine Sophie Barat,
 Bede 25
Philip Neri, Augustine of
 Canterbury 26
Bernard of Montjoux 28
Joan of Arc 30

JUNE
Justin 1
Martyrs of Uganda 3
Boniface 5
Martha (East) 6
Columba of Iona 9
Antony of Padua 13
Thomas More 22
John the Baptist 24
Peter and Paul 29

JULY
Thomas 3
Athanasius the Aconite 5
Benedict 11
Mary Magdalene 22
Bridget of Sweden 23
Christopher, James the Great 25

Anne (West) 26
Martha (West) 29
Ignatius of Loyola 31

AUGUST
Jean-Baptiste Vianney 4
Fourteen Holy Helpers,
    Dominic 8
Edith Stein 9
Clare of Assisi 11
Maximilian Kolbe 14
Mary, the Blessed Virgin
    (Assumption) 15
Stephen of Hungary 16
Rose of Lima 23
Augustine of Hippo 28

SEPTEMBER
Gregory the Great 3
John Chrysostom (West) 13
Hildegard of Bingen 17
Matthew 21
Padre Pio 23
Sergius of Radonezh, Firmin 25
Wenceslas 28
Archangel Michael 29

Below The running of the bulls in Pamplona takes place on 7 July, the day the relics of St Fermin, a popular local saint, came to the town.

Above St Athanasius the Aconite, a Greek Father of the Church (print, 16th century). His feast day is 5 July.

OCTOBER
Theresa of Lisieux 1
Francis of Assisi 4
Denys of Paris, Martyrs of
    the Spanish Civil War 9
Edward the Confessor 13
Theresa of Ávila 15
Luke 18
Crispin and Crispinian 25
Simon, Jude 28

NOVEMBER
All Saints 1
All Souls 2
Malachy 3
Vincent Liem 7
Leo the Great (West) 10
Martin of Tours (West) 11
John Chrysostom (East) 13
Albert the Great 15
Elizabeth of Hungary 17
Cecilia 22
Alexander Nevski 23
Andrew 30

DECEMBER
Francis Xavier 3
Nicholas of Myra 6
Ambrose (West) 7
Eulalia of Mérida 10
Lucy 13
John of the Cross 14
Thomas 21
Stephen (West) 26
John 27
Holy Innocents (West) 28, (East) 9
Thomas Becket 29

Below The Feast of St Lucy (Carl Larsson, 20th century). On 13 December, the oldest girl in a Scandinavian family wears a crown of candles.

HEROES AND MARTYRS

REVERENCE FOR RELICS AND DEEP ATTACHMENT TO THE SAINTS DID NOT SIT WELL WITH ALL BELIEVERS. PROTESTANTS REGARDED THESE PASSIONS AS IDOLATRY, AN AFFRONT TO THE TRUE FAITH, AND THREW OUT THE SAINTS. YET THE IDEA OF HONOURING HEROES REMAINS.

For more than a thousand years, Christendom guarded and reigned over Europe, Russia and Eastern Europe. The pope, his bishops, archbishops and clergy played a major role in economic and political life. The vast majority of the people recognized the authority of the Church. Even kings and queens, believed to be anointed by God to rule, formed an integral part of the system.

But by the 14th century, the Church was not the fervent, disciplined institution it once had been. Popes lived in splendour and

Below Protestant Martin Luther is shown here in triumph over Catholic Pope Leo X (woodcut, 1568).

priests were corruptible. The Reformation started as a call to return to the "purity" of early Christianity, and was not intended to create a major rift. However, great differences of opinion arose, and during the 15th and 16th centuries Christendom became a realm of war and disorder.

CRY FOR REFORM

Reformers insisted the individual was important to God and no person needed the intercession of saints or priests to reach him. They insisted that veneration of the saints was contrary to the teachings of the Bible. As a result, the Protestants, as reformers came to be known, refuted the need for

Above A portrait of Martin Luther, the priest who started the Protestant movement (Lucas Cranach, the Elder, 1529). He is greatly honoured for his brave and radical reforms.

saints as intermediaries, and dismissed the rule that priests be ordained by the pope. In acts of rebellion against the Roman Church, Protestants in countries across northern Europe forbade all worship relating to saints: relics, shrines and pilgrimages

were all considered unnecessary and banned. Even images of the Blessed Virgin were prohibited.

EVENTS IN ENGLAND

However, the Church of England was born out of political need rather than religious fervour. Henry VIII (1491–1547) chafed under papal rule and rejected the authority of Rome.

A period of killings and torture of Roman Catholics under Henry was followed by a similar persecution of Protestants by Mary Tudor (1516–58). By the death of Elizabeth I in 1603, most English subjects had learnt to accept that their monarch, and not the pope, was the head of their Church. However, English Protestants did not reject all the practices of the Roman Church. Indeed, in the Preface to their new Book of Common Prayer, the English Church emphasized the continuation of "the main essentials".

Priests continued to be ordained (though not by the pope), and the saints were not abandoned. The English simply decided not to create any more. Their Church proclaimed that images, relics and the "invocation of the saints is a fond thing vainly invented…but rather repugnant to the Word of God".

CATHOLIC CUSTOMS

Despite this general antipathy towards sainthood, the English Church does acknowledge feast days for the Blessed Virgin and the apostles in the Book of Common Prayer. Obscure regional customs also hint at an English attachment to the old saints.

For instance, in Derbyshire, to avoid the charge of idolatry, it was rumoured that people would create temporary icons of the saints. It is thought that in former remote places, such as Buxton,

Eyam and Tideswell, the villagers dressed the village wells with intricate images of flowers that represented an apostle, a saint or the Blessed Virgin. These decorations appeared on the feast days.

The habit of honouring the most devout Christians in the community was hard to abandon, too. Consequently, in rejecting the title of saint, the Church of England chose instead to define such people as "Heroes and Martyrs". On 9 July 1998, Queen Elizabeth II, Supreme Head of the Church of England, accompanied by the highest priestly officer of her Church, the Archbishop of Canterbury, unveiled ten statues of 20th-century martyrs. The list was cross-denominational, and in fact none of the men and women so honoured were members of the Church of England.

20TH-CENTURY MARTYRS

Instead of saints, the Church of England recognized heroes and martyrs. Statues of ten heroes and martyrs were erected on the façade of Westminster Abbey in London.

Grand Duchess Elizabeth of Russia: Murdered in 1918 during the Russian Revolution.
Manche Masemola: Killed in 1928 by her parents in South Africa for converting to Christianity.
Maximilian Kolbe: Polish priest murdered in 1941 in a Nazi concentration camp.
Lucian Tapiedi: Peasant from Papua New Guinea murdered in 1942 by Japanese troops.
Dietrich Bonhoeffer: German pastor murdered in 1945 by the Nazis.
Janani Luwum: Teacher murdered in 1977 by Idi Amin in Uganda.
Esther John: Indian missionary martyred in 1960.
Dr Martin Luther King Jr: Civil rights campaigner assassinated in 1968 in the USA.
Wang Zhiming: Chinese pastor killed in 1973 by the government.
Archbishop Oscar Romero: Murdered in 1980 in San Salvador.

Above The martyrs' statues at Westminster Abbey: Martin Luther King Jr, Oscar Romero, Dietrich Bonhoeffer, Esther John and Lucian Tapiedi.

NEW WORLDS

EXPLORATIONS BEYOND EUROPE HELPED SPREAD THE CHRISTIAN FAITH TO THE AMERICAS, AFRICA, INDIA AND THE FAR EAST. MISSIONARIES AND THEIR CONVERTS FACED HARDSHIP, EVEN MARTYRDOM, AND INEVITABLY THE COMPANY OF SAINTS EXPANDED.

The apostles set a pattern of evangelism, making it a duty for Christians to spread the Gospel. Whether Roman Catholic, Eastern Orthodox or Protestant, churches have always treated this duty as a serious commitment.

The faith of these missionaries was tested during the widespread explorations of the Europeans in the 17th and 18th centuries. Adventurers and merchants first traded with, then colonized, far-flung lands, and Christian evangelists followed in their wake.

MISSIONARY MARTYRS

Modern secular opinion asserts that these missions forced their faith on people for mere political purpose or to exploit natural resources. This may be true of

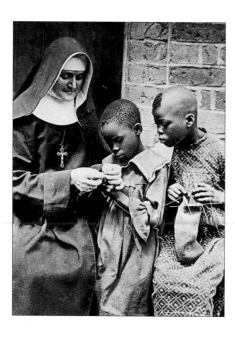

Below A Catholic nun in Africa teaches children how to use knitting needles during the 1920s.

ambitious leaders, but thousands of lowly religious gave their lives to the service of the indigenous people of these lands. Frequently, the missionaries protected their flock from both colonial masters and local warlords.

In remote, uncharted parts of the world, nuns and monks from Ireland, France, Portugal and Spain suffered the same hardship as their flock. They also filled non-religious roles as nurses and educators. Many paid the ultimate price of martyrdom and were canonized for their faith.

St Francis Xavier was among the first to be venerated for his life as an evangelist beyond the bounds of old Christendom. He travelled through the Far East, spreading the gospel, and was martyred. As other Europeans followed his example through the Americas, Asia and Africa, so the company of saints expanded.

NATIVE CONVERTS

The legends of the saints were told to inspire converts and it mattered not that the Blessed Virgin was depicted with Chinese or Mexican features. With the infant in her arms, she became a universal symbol. Regardless of ethnic features, St Francis was recognized with his stigmata, and St Roch with the dog at his feet.

One of the earliest New World converts to inspire a cultus was Blessed Kateri Tekakwitha, a Native American who died in 1680 and was beatified in 1980. Similarly, a cultus developed after

Above A Chinese representation of The Nativity (Lu-Hang-Hien, 19th century).

the death of the Spanish Dominican St Joachim Royo, who died in China in 1748.

In Japan, Paul Miki and his companions, converts of St Francis Xavier, suffered relentless persecution before finally being tortured and crucified in 1597. Survivors venerated the blood-stained clothes of these 26 victims who were all canonized.

In Uganda, Charles Lwanga and his 21 companions, all under the age of 25, were burned alive for their faith in the 1880s. As they faced their horrific deaths, "their exemplary courage and cheerfulness were comparable with those of the early Christians". They were canonized in 1964.

The first native saint of the USA, Elizabeth Seton, died in 1821, and was canonized only in 1971 for her charity towards deprived children.

St Josephine Bakhita was taken into slavery in Africa, but found refuge in a convent in Italy. Her

Right Missionaries and their catechumens experience floodwater in Hindustan, north India, in 1910.

work as a nurse, together with her humility, attracted a cultus after she died in 1947. She was canonized in 2000.

MASS CANONIZATION

Pope John Paul II recognized the neglected martyrs of the New and Developing Worlds. Tireless in visiting Catholic communities and in reinforcing the Universal Church, the late pope created more than 480 new saints. Through this pope's concern for his global flock, victims of mass persecution have been sanctified. He canonized 117 martyrs of Vietnam, all of whom gave their lives between 1745 and 1862. The Martyrs of Mexico, 25 Christians killed between 1915 and 1937, were also made saints in 2000.

Furthermore, he initiated the process of sanctification of the estimated 6,832 priests and religious put to death during the Spanish Civil War (1936–39). By creating native sainthoods, the pope hoped to encourage the Church in those parts.

Above A painting of the Madonna on animal hide, made by Pueblo Indians in a traditional style (1675).

Left An armed ship carrying missionaries under the monogram of Jesus off the coast of New Granada, modern-day Colombia (artist unknown, 18th century).

MODERN PILGRIMS

THE MODERN ERA HAS SEEN A REVIVAL IN PILGRIMAGE AS A
CHRISTIAN DUTY. NOT SINCE THE 16TH-CENTURY REFORMATION
OF THE CHURCH HAVE SO MANY PILGRIMS UNDERTAKEN THE LONG
JOURNEYS TO SHRINES FOR CURES, PENANCE AND PRAYER.

The pious duty of pilgrimage, although never abandoned by Roman Catholics, regained some of its former popularity during the Victorian era. The Ottoman Islamic hold on Palestine had weakened, and in 1855 a cross was borne through Jerusalem for the first time since the Crusades.

Pilgrims began visiting again the holy sites of Jerusalem, Bethlehem and Nazareth. By 1900, the traveller Gertrude Bell described a hostelry "packed with pilgrims tight as herrings sleeping in rows on the floor".

VISIONS OF MARY

Various extraordinary events have contributed to this latter-day increase in the popularity of saints. In 1876, more than 100,000 pilgrims attended the dedication of the church at Lourdes, in south-west France, where St Bernadette received a vision of the Virgin Mary. Three years later, at Knock in Ireland, 15 people saw a vision standing on the village chapel roof of the Virgin accompanied by St Joseph, St John and a lamb. A shrine there now attracts more than a million pilgrims every year.

In 1917, the Blessed Virgin was said to have visited three children at Fátima in Portugal and entrusted them with three secrets. Now five million pilgrims a year visit their shrine. Believers claim that the Virgin told the children about forthcoming mass death in a second world war and an

Below Catholic pilgrims during the Holy Week praying at the first Station of the Cross on the Via Dolorosa in Jerusalem (Erich Matson, c.1900).

Above Pope John Paul II celebrated mass with a million believers in front of a statue of the Virgin in Fátima, Portugal, on 12 May 1991.

attempted assassination of a pope – both of which prophecies have come true.

ECHOES OF THE PAST

Modern pilgrims, in imitation of the difficult conditions of their medieval counterparts, and also to show penitence, may choose to walk the "pilgrim's way" to particular shrines.

A popular route is the trek to Santiego de Compostela on the Atlantic coast of Spain. During their journey, they may pass other

places of pilgrimage, such as the shrine to the Virgin Mary in Vézelay and at Conques, and can see the relics of the martyr, St Foy.

The main aim of the pilgrimage is to visit the tomb and relics of St James the Great at Santiago de Compostela. The Church gives a certificate to those pilgrims who have walked the last 100km/ 60 miles or cycled the last 200km/ 120 miles of the route. These awards echo the medieval habit of rewarding successful pilgrims with distinctive clothes and badges.

RECENT DEVELOPMENTS

Ever since 1717, the most devout have walked about 110km/70 miles from Warsaw to the Jasna Gora monastery in Poland to see the miraculous icon of Our Lady of Czestochowa, reputedly painted by St Luke. But since the ending of Communist rule in the late 20th century, many more throng the route. An estimated million pilgrims a year now go to the site.

The biggest crowds are found at Zihuatanejo in Guadalupe, Mexico, where St Juan Diego had a vision of the Virgin. Ten million pilgrims pay homage to Our Lady of Guadalupe at this shrine every year. And seven million people travel to the tomb of the humble stigmatic, St Padre Pio, at San Giovanni Rotondo in south Italy.

PERSONAL JOURNEYS

Other holy sites and shrines draw those seeking a significance particular to themselves. The pilgrim might be named after the saint, or be seeking one who is patron of a disease or other affliction.

Many visit Assisi, Italy, for St Francis, although an earthquake has left this site damaged. Pilgrims travel to the abbeys at Montserrat in France, or Trier in Germany, to seek intercession from the saints and wonder at the glorious holy

BEING A PILGRIM

Modern Roman Catholic and Orthodox pilgrims are serious in their intent when they undertake journeys to the places associated with the saints. This is often the site where their relics are enshrined. Pilgrims seek penance and offer prayers of gratitude, or request their intercession.

Walking the route to a shrine, the faithful will take time to pray or undergo some physical hardship in penance. They venerate those shrines they pass as they head toward their final destination. If that is Rome, they will climb, on hands and knees, the hard marble steps of the Holy Stairs of St Peter's Cathedral.

Popular pilgrimages are those to Assisi, the shrine of St Francis, or to places that honour St James the Great in South America, or visits to sacred sites of the Holy Land. But in the 21st century, the sites and festivals that attract most visitors are those associated with the Virgin Mary, the one figure from the company of saints who seems to have sustained an imaginative hold on believers – and non-believers.

Above Pilgrims kneel with crosses at the pass of Roncesvalles, Spain, on their way from south-west France to Santiago de Compostela.

buildings. Today, pilgrimages to the Holy Land have become almost as dangerous as they were during the Crusades.

Many aspects of modern pilgrimage resemble the medieval experience, as Chaucer described in his poetic work *The Canterbury Tales*. Hostelries proliferate along the routes, especially near the shrines, just as they did in the Middle Ages. Translators and guides find work, while merchants are busy selling souvenirs, often facsimiles of medieval relics.

Right Souvenir of the pilgrimage to Lourdes, made for the International Exhibition in Paris in 1867.

THE BLESSED

THE CHURCH DOES NOT GRANT SAINTHOOD LIGHTLY. HOLY SOULS MAY REMAIN FOR DECADES, EVEN CENTURIES, IN THE RANKS OF THE BLESSED OR THE VENERABLE, WHILE THE CLAIMS MADE ON THEIR BEHALF ARE CAREFULLY SCRUTINIZED BY THE VATICAN.

Above A photo of Blessed Father Joseph Damien de Veuster in 1873.

Mother Teresa of Calcutta lived a life that even the secular acknowledge was saintly. In the minds of many believers she is a saint. Yet she has not been canonized. Until a second miracle is officially attributed to her, she remains among the Blessed. Likewise, in the Rotunda of the Capitol Building in Washington, D.C., USA, stands a statue of the Blessed Father Joseph Damien de Veuster. This man was, and still is, deeply venerated by lepers and their families. For 16 years he nursed the lepers of Moloka'i in Hawaii. His gentle devotion and Christian faith were recognized as being worthy of a saint. He died in 1889 and was eventually beatified in 1995 by Pope John Paul II, but Catholics in Hawaii already regard Father Damien as a fully fledged saint.

UNKNOWN BUT HOLY

These are but two individuals who led lives of public service. Many others do not have national or global recognition. Cultuses have sometimes asked for obscure, private individuals to be named as saints. One such is Pierre Toussaint who was born a slave in Haiti in 1776 and taken by his master, John Berard, to live with him in New York. There Berard taught Pierre to read and write.

When Berard died, Pierre continued to care for the family of his late master by working as a barber. When Mrs Berard married again, Pierre set up his own home and with his wife cared for the homeless and destitute.

They purchased the freedom of many slaves, opened a school, and set up a religious order for black

Left The procession of the Beatified in The Last Judgement (Giotto di Bondone, 1303).

women. After his death in 1853, Toussaint became the only layman to be buried in the grand precincts of St Patrick's Cathedral in New York. He was recognized as Venerable by the Church in 1996, but in the local community people know him fondly as the "Barber Saint".

Left A watercolour portrait of Pierre Toussaint, fondly known as the "Barber Saint" (c.1825).

WILD MYSTIC

An Indian girl, Kateri Tekakwitha, endured a short wretched life, spent poor and lonely. Her father was a Mohawk chief and her parents died of smallpox. She survived but was scarred and left partially blind. Yet she claimed always to be filled with the joy of her faith.

Kateri, a mystic, revelled in the great prairie wilderness that was her home. She came to be known as the "Lily of the Mohawks", though some called her the "Mystic of the Wilds".

When she died in 1680, the local Jesuit missionaries were astounded to find her corpse transformed into the gracious form of a beautiful young woman. Their witness to her devotion and spiritual power formed the ground for her being granted beatification in 1980.

Right A statue of Blessed Kateri Tekakwitha, a Native American mystic who died in 1680.

PATRONS OF CAUSES

In some cases, the Blessed have been allowed to become patrons of causes. Maria Teresa Ledóchowska, who was born into a 19th-century noble Polish family, nevertheless devoted herself to mission work, especially to the abolition of slavery. The countess founded a community, first called the Sodality, now known as the Institute of St Peter Claver. Having taken vows as a nun, Maria worked tirelessly against slavery. She was beatified in 1976 by Pope Paul VI who declared her the patron of Polish missions.

Many saints are honoured for giving to the poor, but Blessed Bernardino of Feltre (d.1494) helped those too proud to accept welfare. He took over the Church's faltering little pawnshops, the *montes pietatis*, started in 1462 by Barnabas of Terni. Under Bernardino's care, the pawnshops were properly run and became very successful. They charged very low rates of interest and profits were used for charity. For centuries the shops could be found all over western Europe. His cultus was approved in 1728.

MOTHER TERESA OF CALCUTTA

Even as a small child in Skopje, Macedonia, Teresa showed a religious turn of mind and, at 17, announced she wanted to become a missionary. She was sent to India and took her vows as a nun in 1937.

Teresa worked as a teacher until 1946, when she claimed she heard the voice of Jesus calling for her help. Further voices told her to found the Missionaries of Charity. For the rest of her life she devoted her energies to the care of the ill and dying poor of Calcutta.

So inspirational was her example that her followers opened other centres of Missionaries of Charity, first in Venezuela and Tanzania, then in other countries. Women took vows as nuns, and laymen were encouraged to help. Later the Missionaries of Charity Brothers was founded for priests. Mother Teresa died in 1997 and her tomb in Calcutta is a site of pilgrimage. She was beatified in 2002.

Below Mother Teresa in Calcutta, India, in 1976.

ALL SAINTS AND ALL SOULS

THE CHURCH CREATED TWO UNIVERSAL FEAST DAYS TO HONOUR THOSE WHO HAVE LEFT THIS WORLD. CATHOLICS COMMEMORATE ALL SAINTS ON 1 NOVEMBER, AND ALL THE DEVOUT SOULS WHO HAVE NOT YET REACHED HEAVEN THE FOLLOWING DAY.

Precisely when the Roman Catholic Church adopted the practice of commemorating all the saints is unknown. However, it is known that the earliest believers left inscriptions of general prayers for the dead in the catacombs of Rome. Two later saints, St Ephrem (d.AD 373) and St John Chrysostom (d.AD 407), describe in vague terms prayers for "the martyrs of the whole world". Yet, whether these prayers referred only to officially sanctified individuals or more generally to all devout souls who reside in heaven is unclear.

A 7th-century AD manuscript states that not only unknown martyrs but unnamed saints, too, were remembered in prayers and rituals. Catholics believe, to paraphrase St Paul's words, that many of the faithful live not as themselves but through Christ who lives within them. These

Above A man lights a candle at the All Saints Memorial, to celebrate fallen soldiers on Hungarian territory.

Below All Souls' Day in the Churchyard at Glendalough (Joseph Peacock, 19th century).

souls, it is believed, reside in heaven but they are unknown. By the 9th century, the practice of praying to unknown saints had become widespread, and an official feast day was established on 1 November as All Saints, which is known also in England as All Hallows.

ALL SOULS' DAY

Believers pitied the faithful dead who might not be in heaven. Naturally, the living prayed for their dead relatives, priests and friends, in the belief that their prayers would help accelerate the passage of their beloved up to heaven. The faithful prayed for the purification of the souls of their beloved ones and their quick passage through purgatory. According to Roman Catholic belief, this is a transitionary abode where those souls who are not saints wait for redemption before passing to heaven. They depend for that redemption on the prayers of the living.

The origin of offering prayers for the unredeemed may date to before the 7th century. Certainly during the lifetime of Isidore of Seville (*c.*AD 560–636), prayers for this purpose were offered in churches. However, the Roman Church was reluctant to dedicate a liturgical place to those who hover on the edge of heaven.

It was not until the 10th century that the liturgy became fixed. According to tradition, a pilgrim returning from the Holy Land encountered a beggar who pointed to flames issuing from a fissure in the earth, believed to emanate from hell. Despairing moans of the dead were said to be audible. The pilgrim reported his terrible experience to St Odilo, abbot of Cluny, who immediately decreed that a day should be marked for "all the dead who have existed from the beginning of the world to the end of time". The feast day was set on 2 November to commemorate all dead souls.

CAKES FOR THE DEAD

Some have interpreted All Souls' Day in a more sinister light. They see the occasion as a time when the souls of the unredeemed return, briefly, to haunt the living. The angry dead, unsupported by prayers from their relatives and friends, turn into toads or witches to punish the living.

In parts of Catholic Italy, the dead are placated with alms in the form of food left on windowsills or the kitchen table, and bunches of flowers are heaped at gravesides in honour of the dead. In Poland, candles are lit on graves in the cemeteries and bread is left shaped in the figure of a body. In Ireland, the devout celebrate the eve of All Souls with a big feast, but the next day is spent fasting, with flowers laid on graves at cemeteries.

All Souls' Day has developed to become a time for feeding the poor and giving to charity. For centuries, believers in the Church of England used to offer alms to the poor on this day. Children would make lanterns from root vegetables, such as turnips, and go "souling" at the doors of friends and neighbours, asking for spiced buns known as soul-cakes.

The modern, secular world has added its own "spin" on these occasions. Halloween, a hybrid of All Saints and All Souls, has become a time for children to dress up in costumes and act as spooks, with rewards of sweets and money replacing traditional soul-cakes. These particular celebrations originated in the USA, but they have spread to areas where the Church is not as influential as it once was.

THE DAY OF THE DEAD

Catholics in Mexico have turned the period between 31 October and 2 November into a bizarrely festive occasion. A once pre-Hispanic festival merged with the Christian calendar to produce what is known as the "Day of the Dead". On this public holiday people have picnics in the cemeteries, where graves are festooned with flowers, such as marigolds, and candlelight illuminates the scene.

Everywhere on display are skeletons – not real ones, but puppets made of plastic or metal; even cakes are shaped as ornamental skulls. This is not a sad occasion because the devout believe that the dead are all together. It is thought the spirits of the dead may even be hungry when they visit earth on this day, so food is laid at the graves among the flowers for them to eat.

Above At a cemetery in La Digue, Seychelles, visitors bring gifts and flowers to dress the gravestones of their loved ones on All Souls' Day.

THE ROLES OF SAINTS

During the long and complex history of Christianity, saint-hood has been invested with many different meanings. Close to God, saints are thought to be able to act as intermediaries between the human and divine. This combines with the human achievements of the saints to make them examplars of virtue that the faithful can turn to in times of need.

The relevance of saints for particular people, professions and countries is reflected in the adoption of "patron" saints. Another important role of saints has been in the religious orders some have established, reformed or supported, orders that have had lasting influence on the theological and social work of the Church throughout the centuries. Some saints have also had earthly power, as warriors, kings and popes, or as the inspiration for political reform or care and welfare for the sick and poor.

This chapter examines these religious and social roles, including the importance to the faithful of the Holy Family, child saints, the apostles and in later years the mystical help of the Fourteen Helpers, set up by the Pope to send help and comfort in the terrible days of the Black Death. Saints are depicted in some of the world's greatest works of art, and this chapter is illustrated with the paintings that believers feel will help them be drawn closer to the Divine.

Left St Francis Expels the Devils from Arezzo *(Giotto di Bondone, c.1297–1299).*

Top *A bejewelled casket containing the relics of Thomas Becket (c.1190).*

THE HOLY FAMILY

JOSEPH, MARY AND THE INFANT JESUS MAKE UP THE HOLY FAMILY.
THE GOSPEL OF MATTHEW SAYS THAT THE MESSIAH WILL BE
DESCENDED FROM THE HOUSE OF DAVID.

Joseph and Mary were humble and loving parents of the infant Jesus. They brought up their son in the Jewish faith and Jesus was taught to be a carpenter by his earthly father, Joseph.

OF ROYAL DESCENT?
In the first 16 verses of his gospel, Matthew demonstrates a direct line of descent from King David of the Israelites to Joseph and Jesus. Such an ancestry was essential if the Jewish prophecy that the Messiah would come from the House of David was to be fulfilled. The same royal connections are ascribed to Mary, although nothing is known of her origins. Details of the lives of her mother, Anne, and of her father, Joachim, come only from apocryphal sources.

THE BIRTH OF JESUS
When the Roman authorities held a census of the population, Joseph was obliged to travel to

Above The Holy Family
(Luca Signorelli, 1486–90).
Christ is shown as a diligent child.

Below A fresco depicting The Flight into Egypt, *from the Lower Church at Assisi in Italy (Giotto di Bondone, 14th century).*

Bethlehem, the city of David, to record his name. The journey was slow because of his young wife's pregnancy. Mary was very close to giving birth, but as Joseph hurried round Bethlehem at nightfall all he heard was the cry, "No room at the inn". Many other people had crowded into the town to fulfil the Romans' demands.

At last, a kindly innkeeper led him to the stables and told the tired girl that she could rest there. It was here in the stable, alongside cows and donkeys, that Mary gave birth to Jesus and laid him in a manger for lack of a cradle.

Shepherds arrived because angels had told them to visit the new Messiah. A bright star hung over the stable and guided the shepherds who brought the baby the gift of a lamb. The Holy Family received more guests with the arrival some time later of the three Magi, or wise men. They had read signs and warnings that told them where to find the new "King of the Jews". They brought him costly gifts of gold, frankincense and myrrh.

Below Stained glass showing the holy family in the carpenter's shop, Steeple Aston, England (19th century).

Above A Nativity scene from the Bellieu Orthodox Church in Samokov, Bulgaria (16th century).

After Jesus was born, Joseph received a warning that Herod was planning to kill the baby, so the Holy Family fled to Egypt. Herod carried out his threat, killing all male infants in Bethlehem under two years, but the Holy Infant was not among them.

NO ORDINARY CHILD

Because the archangel Gabriel had appeared to both Mary, at the Annunciation, and to Joseph to explain the importance of their son, they knew that Jesus was a special child. In spite of this they were still horrified to find, a day

into their return journey from the annual trip to Jerusalem for Passover, that the 12-year-old Jesus could not be found among the family group.

Joseph and Mary returned immediately to the city and after searching for three days found him in the temple in the midst of doctors and rabbis, listening to the teachings and asking questions. Jesus calmly asked his mother why she had been so worried when she knew that he would be "about my Father's business".

THE CRUCIFIXION

We know from St John's Gospel that the Blessed Virgin was accompanied by her sister, Mary of Cleophas during her vigil at the foot of the cross. As Jesus hung from the cross, he asked the apostle John to care for his mother. This implies that she had no other sons or a husband to care for her after Jesus' death. By tradition Mary became surrogate mother to John, and travelled with him on missionary work abroad.

Below Twelve-year-old Jesus debating with the rabbis in the temple (Adolph Friedrich Erdmann von Menzel, 1851).

THE APOSTLES

THE 12 MEN CHOSEN BY JESUS TO AID HIM IN HIS WORK WENT OUT TO PREACH THE GOSPEL WITH AUTHORITY AFTER HIS DEATH. IT WAS EACH APOSTLE'S DUTY TO LIVE IN IMITATION OF CHRIST.

Above A very early fresco of Jesus Christ and his apostles, found in a church in Cappadocia, Turkey.

Jesus had at least 120, possibly thousands, of disciples. They were ordinary men and women who followed him wherever he went, learning from his teachings. He selected 12 special men to be his apostles (derived from the Greek word for "ambassador") from among these people. They became his closest companions and were witness to some of the most significant moments of Christ's life and resurrection.

FOLLOWERS OF JESUS

The earliest followers of Christ were two pairs of brothers – Peter and Andrew, and James and John – fishermen who worked along the coast of the Sea of Galilee. Tax collectors were generally despised at the time, and yet that was the profession of Matthew, the next apostle to be called.

It is thought that 11 of these 12 men were Galileans. Judas Iscariot, their treasurer and the man who betrayed Jesus, was the only non-Galilean. After the Crucifixion, Peter oversaw the replacement of Judas by Matthias.

FISHERS OF MEN

When Jesus called Peter and Andrew he said that if they followed him he would make them "fishers of men". Many Christians consider these words to be a metaphor for the apostles' role: to bring people to Jesus as a fisherman catches fish.

In the years of persecution, cautious Christians used the image of a fish, scratched on walls and rocks, as a secret sign. *Icthys*, the Greek word for "fish", is an acrostic, or word puzzle, consisting of the initial letters for five other words that described Christ to his believers: *Iesous Christos Theou Yios Soter* (Jesus Christ, Son of God, Saviour).

ROLE OF THE APOSTLES

Jesus defined the purpose of the work of his chosen few. They were to teach his message, to baptize, to rule by guiding the faithful, and to sanctify the grace of God through prayer. These roles were to be passed on to successors when an apostle died or became frail.

Roman Catholics believe that Jesus appointed these "men of the apostolate" to administer his Church. He put the organization into their hands with Peter, the first pope, as his chief. Peter was to rule the whole Church, make judgements and name his successor. This division of duties has remained the basis of the administrative structure of the Church ever since. All popes are believed to be Peter's successors.

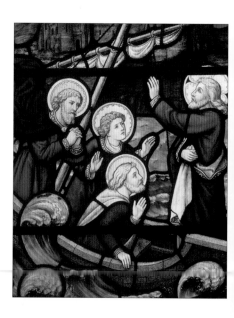

Above Christ calming a storm and saving fishermen in stained glass from Exeter Cathedral, England.

JUDAS ISCARIOT

This apostle is infamous for betraying Christ to the Jewish authorities. But it was his method of identifying his leader, Jesus, that is perceived as particularly repugnant. Judas knew that Jesus and the apostles had spent the night praying in the garden of Gethsemane. At dawn, he and the temple guards approached the group, and Judas told the guards, "The one I kiss is the man you want". For the sum of 30 pieces of silver, he kissed Jesus, who was then led to his death.

It was said that Judas, crazed with remorse, threw the "blood money" into the temple and then hanged himself. The kind of tree to which he tied his noose is still known as a Judas tree, and the field where Judas died is called "Áceldama" – the field of blood. His name is given to traitors, while any act of betrayal is often termed "the kiss of Judas".

Right The traitor's kiss is hewn from stone on this church wall in France.

Protestants were, and are, more ambivalent about the role of the individual apostles. Some credit them with divine authority. Other sects say they are simply the first evangelists or preachers. They are seen as early missionaries who were given significant qualities to fulfil their role as heralds of the gospel message.

SPREADING THE WORD

Soon after he had chosen the 12, Jesus gave his apostles the power to cast out evil spirits and cure disease. He sent them out in pairs to preach and use their gifts in the towns of Galilee, instructing them to "take nothing for their journey, except a mere staff".

After the Resurrection, the apostles dedicated themselves to spreading the teachings of Jesus around the known world. Peter was the first of them to perform a miracle and was also one of the first apostles to set out into the world as a missionary.

All the apostles undertook arduous journeys to fulfil their appointed roles. They set high standards of obedience, poverty and chastity, avoiding all worldly pleasures that might distract them from their mission.

DYING FOR THEIR FAITH

Such was the conviction of these men that they were prepared to die cruel deaths for their faith. A total of 11 apostles were martyred. The work of these brave men proved productive. After 300 years of continued apostleship the Emperor Constantine I made Christianity the religion of the Roman Empire, and from then on the "new" religion spread rapidly.

Below All the apostles were present with Jesus at the Last Supper (Justus van Gent, 1473–74).

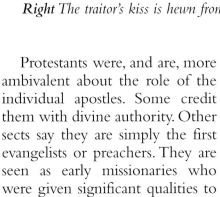

CHILD SAINTS

THOUSANDS OF CHILDREN HAVE DIED IN DEFENCE OF THEIR FAITH, INDIVIDUALLY OR ALONGSIDE THEIR CHRISTIAN FAMILIES. YET FEW NAMES SURVIVE FROM THIS GROUP OF YOUNG MARTYR SAINTS.

Many children were named as saints not only for the purity and innocence of their youth, but for the horrible deaths they suffered as martyrs.

It is safe to assume that thousands of unnamed children, together with their families, were slaughtered by the Roman authorities. Some attracted a cultus and their names live on. These children mostly come from the early years of the faith when its members were subject to horrific, intermittent persecution.

EARLY MARTYRS

Legend describes St Foy (or Faith) as a defiant child who is said to have lived in Agen, Gaul (France) in the late 3rd century. Legend states that she was roasted alive and beheaded for her belief. Her bravery was venerated and thousands made the journey to visit her relics in Conques, France. Crusader soldiers, especially, pleaded for her protection.

The story of St Irene tells that this brave Macedonian girl was about 13 when she was arrested with her sisters

Above The Abbey church of St Foy in Conques, France, which holds her gorgeous relics.

in *c.*AD 303. While her sisters were killed, Irene was spared because she was so young. She was sent naked into the soldiers' brothel where no man dared approach her. She was eventually burnt alive in AD 304.

Although the 4th-century St Pelagia of Antioch is named in the church litany, all we know about her is that, when she was 15, soldiers invaded her home. To escape from them and avoid dishonour, the young virgin sacrificed her life by jumping off the roof of her house.

St Philomena's history is also obscure, but even now pilgrims visit her shrine in Naples. Her relics were unearthed in 1802 near an inscription bearing her name in the Roman catacombs. Her relics were subsequently moved to Naples, and miracles began to occur.

Because of controversy surrounding the relics of St Philomena, in 1961 the Holy See removed her from the liturgical calendar of saints and wanted to dismantle her shrine; yet she continues to attract pilgrims.

Son of Coenwulf, King of Mercia (AD 796–821), Prince Kenelm was next in line for the throne. But according to legend his sister, Quendreda, was jealous of the seven-year-old Christian prince and ordered the boy's tutor to murder him so she would inherit the throne. It was said that a dove carried a document to Rome telling of his death, and his relics were translated to Winchcombe in Gloucestershire. His wicked sister's eyes fell out and she was blind for the rest of her life.

Left A sculpture of St Philomena made out of gilded wood (1890).

CHILD MARTYRS

Names with age at death; those in bold refer to martyrs described on these two pages:

Agape (Charity), 9
Agnes, 13
Christodoulos, 14
Dominic Savio, 15
Elpis (Hope), 10
Eulalia Mérida, 12
Foy (or **Faith**), unknown
Gabriel Gowdel, 7
Irene, 13
Justus of Beauvais, 9
Kenelm, 7
Kizito, 13
Maria Goretti, 12
Niño de Atocha, unknown
Pancras of Rome, 14
Paul Lang Fu, 9
Pelagia of Antioch, 15
Philomena, unknown
Pistis (Faith), 12
Rais, 12

Right Maria Goretti was canonized by Pope Pius XII at St Peter's in Rome in 1950.

19TH AND 20TH CENTURIES

There are only a few known child saints from the 19th and 20th centuries. They are symbols of the bravery of the thousands of unnamed children who suffered for their faith during this time.

One such child is Dominic Savio. He was only 12 when he entered a Turin monastery. A cheerful, peaceful child, he was famous for the hours he spent in prayer. Dominic suffered from tuberculosis and, during a fever, experienced a vision. Before his death in 1857 he cried out, "I am seeing the most wonderful things!" He was 15.

During the Boxer Rebellion in 1900, thousands of Christians were murdered for playing a part in the foreign domination of China. One of the youngest was Paul Lang Fu, just nine years old. He ran to his mother's side as soldiers tied her to a tree, but they hacked off his arm and burnt him to death.

Maria Goretti (1890–1902) was a martyr for chastity and the Christian life. She was only 12 years old when she was murdered by a man who tried to rape her. Before she died, she forgave him his sin. He was imprisoned and after eight years he became a Christian; he was present at her canonization in 1950.

AGNES

Agnes is probably the best-known child saint. Some stories claim she was 13 when she died in Rome around AD 305. She was buried on the Via Nomentana, and a church was built over her grave soon after her death.

This young Christian girl refused to marry the son of a Roman prefect because she had dedicated herself to Christ. When the son complained, the father tried to force the marriage. Agnes remained steadfast in her refusal. According to legend she was then dragged naked through the streets to a brothel, but her hair grew and hid her body. One man who tried to rape her was blinded, but Agnes prayed for him and his sight returned. The Romans finally put her to death by piercing her throat with a sword after flames would not burn her.

Agnes is often painted with a lamb to symbolize her purity and every year, on her feast day, two lambs are blessed inside her church in Rome. Their wool is woven by the nuns of St Agnes' convent into bands which the pope confers on bishops as a sign of authority. The superstitious believe virgins who go without supper on the eve of the feast of St Agnes will dream of the man who will become their true love.

Left St Agnes holding the palm of martyrdom (Lucas van Leyden, 1510).

PATRON SAINTS OF PROFESSIONS

IN THE WORLD OF WORK, SOME SAINTS ARE PATRONS BY CUSTOM, OTHERS BY PAPAL CONCESSION. SOME HELPED PARTICULAR PROFESSIONS; OTHERS ARE CHOSEN FOR THE LIVES THEY LED.

Accountants – Matthew
Actors – Genesius of Arles, Vitus
Actresses – Pelagia the Penitent
Advertisers – Bernardino of Siena
Air crew – Joseph of Copertino, Theresa of Lisieux
Anaesthetists – René Goupil
Apothecaries – Nicholas of Myra, Cosmas and Damian
Archaeologists – Jerome, Helen
Architects – Thomas, Barbara
Art dealers – John
Artists – Luke, Catherine de'Vigri of Bologna
Astronauts – Joseph of Copertino
Astronomers – Dominic
Athletes – Sebastian
Authors – John, Paul, Lucy, Francis of Sales
Bakers – Elizabeth of Hungary, Zita, Nicholas of Myra, Agatha
Bankers – Bernardino of Feltre, Matthew
Bar staff – Amand
Basket-makers – Antony of Egypt
Beekeepers – Ambrose, Bernard of Clairvaux, Valentine, Modomnoc
Bishops – Charles Borromeo
Blacksmiths – Dunstan, Eloi
Bookkeepers – Matthew
Brewers – Amand, Wenceslas, Augustine of Hippo, Boniface
Bricklayers – Stephen of Hungary
Broadcasters – Archangel Gabriel
Builders – Barbara, Blaise, Louis IX, Vincent Ferrer
Bus drivers – Christopher
Butchers – Adrian of Nicomedia, Luke
Cab drivers – Christopher, Eloi, Fiacre, Frances of Rome
Cabinet-makers – Anne, Joseph, Victor of Marseilles
Carpenters – Joseph, Thomas
Civil servants – Thomas More

Above St Bernardino of Siena *(Giovanni di Paolo, 1450). He is patron of advertisers.*

Clergy – Gabriel Possenti
Clowns – Genesius of Arles, Julian the Hospitaller
Cobblers – Crispin and Crispinian, Bartholomew
Cooks, chefs – Laurence, Macarius the Younger, Martha, Paschal Baylon
Craftsmen – Eloi, Catherine of Alexandria

Customs officers – Matthew
Dancers – Vitus, Genesius of Arles, Philemon
Dentists – Apollonia
Dietitians – Martha
Diplomats – Archangel Gabriel
Doctors – Blaise, Cosmas and Damian, Pantaleon
Domestic workers – Adelelmus, Martha, Zita
Ecologists – Francis of Assisi
Editors – John Bosco, Francis of Sales
Engineers – Ferdinand III
Farm-workers – Benedict, Isidore the Farmer, Eloi, Phocas of Sinope, George
Firefighters – Agatha, Laurence, Catherine of Siena
Fishermen – Andrew, Peter, Simon, Zeno, Magnus
Florists – Dorothy, Rose of Lima
Funeral directors – Joseph of Arimathea, Dismas, Sebastian

Above St Fiacre *(illumination, 15th century). Cab drivers in Paris plied their trade from the hotel St Fiacre and the saint has become their patron.*

Above St Ivo of Brittany is patron of judges because he mediated in church disputes (Gaudenzio Ferrari, 1520).

Goldsmiths – Dunstan, Eloi
Grocers – Archangel Michael, Leonard of Noblac
Gunners – Barbara
Hairdressers – Louis IX, Martin de Porres, Mary Magdalene
Hoteliers – Amand, Julian the Hospitaller, Martha
Housewives – Martha, Zita, Anne
Huntsmen – Eustace, Hubert
Jewellers – Eloi, Agatha, Dunstan
Journalists – Francis of Sales, Paul, Maximilian Kolbe
Judges – Ivo of Brittany
Labourers – Eloi, Isidore the Farmer, Guy of Anderlecht, Lucy
Lawyers – Ivo of Brittany, Thomas More, Robert Bellarmine
Leather-workers – Crispin and Crispinian, Bartholomew
Librarians – Jerome, Catherine of Alexandria, Laurence of Rome
Locksmiths – Dunstan, Eloi, Peter, Leonard of Noblac
Magistrates – Ferdinand III
Mechanics – Catherine of Alexandria
Merchants – Nicholas, Homobonus
Midwives – Dorothy of Myra,

Right Limestone statue of St Maurice, the patron of soldiers and armies (Magdeburg Cathedral, c.1240).

Brigid of Ireland, Peter of Verona, Raymund Nonnatus
Miners – Barbara
Musicians – Cecilia, Gregory the Great
Naval officers – Francis of Paola
Nurses – Agatha, Camillus of Lellis, John of God, Catherine of Siena
Obstetricians – Raymund Nonnatus
Painters – Catherine de'Vigri of Bologna, Benedict Biscop
Paramedics – Archangel Michael
Paratroopers – Archangel Michael
Pawnbrokers – Nicholas of Myra
Perfumers – Nicholas of Myra, Mary Magdalene
Philosophers – Albert the Great, Justin, Catherine of Alexandria, Thomas Aquinas
Photographers – Veronica
Poets – Columba of Iona, John of the Cross, Brigid of Ireland, Cecilia
Police officers – Archangel Michael, Sebastian
Politicians – Thomas More
Priests – Jean-Baptiste Vianney
Printers – Augustine of Hippo, John of God

Above St Vincent of Saragossa is surrounded by vines and grapes to indicate his patronage of wine-makers.

Publishers – John of God
Sailors – Nicholas of Myra, Francis of Paola, Phocas of Sinope
Scholars – Jerome, Brigid of Ireland, Catherine of Alexandria
Scientists – Albert the Great, Dominic
Secretaries – Genesius of Arles, Catherine of Alexandria
Silversmiths – Andronicus, Dunstan
Social workers – John Francis Regis, Louise de Marillac
Soldiers – Martin of Tours, George, Maurice, Fay, James the Great
Surgeons – Cosmas and Damian, Luke, Roch
Surveyors – Thomas
Tailors – Boniface, Homobonus
Tax collectors – Matthew
Teachers – John-Baptist de la Salle, Catherine of Alexandria, Francis of Sales, Gregory the Great, Ursula
Veterinarians – Eloi, Blaise, James the Great
Waiters – Martha, Notburga, Zita
Weavers – Maurice
Wine-makers – Amand, Vincent of Saragossa, Martin of Tours

RELIGIOUS ORDERS

MONASTERIES AND CONVENTS SUSTAIN COMMUNITIES DEVOTED TO A
STRICT RELIGIOUS LIFE. THESE RELIGIOUS ORDERS HAVE A ROLE IN
ROMAN CATHOLIC AND EASTERN ORTHODOX CHURCHES.

Although Christianity does not regard ownership of property or marriage as sinful, the Church recognizes that some people have a special calling to dedicate their lives to prayer and to God.

Those called to this religious life fall into two categories. The first are the eremites, who choose to pursue a life of solitary meditation, following the precepts formulated by St Antony of Egypt and other Desert Fathers. The second group, the coenobites, share a communal life of prayer that is influenced by the ideas of St Pachomius. Founders of the various orders laid down rules for monastic life, which continue to apply in Roman Catholic and Eastern Orthodox Churches.

The lives of all monks and nuns are guided by the primary disciplines of prayer, spiritual development, inner contemplation and physical labour.

EARLY MODELS

The earliest monasteries were self-supporting and independent of papal authority. Many monks were not even ordained as priests.

Some early founders, such as Martin of Tours and Cassian, maintained harsh regimes. But St Benedict, who established a monastery at Monte Cassino, Italy, rejected this military-like austerity. His rules were those of a well-ordered household with routine and sympathetic discipline. He encouraged labour to sustain the community and literacy to provide an understanding of the scriptures. By the 10th century, his rule was accepted throughout Western Christendom.

The Rule of St Augustine of Canterbury was also influential. He stipulated that monks should be ordained clerics, living within an order but going into the world to work as priests.

Above St Zeno *(Francesco Bonaza, 17th century). St Zeno founded the earliest nunneries and encouraged women to take vows.*

Above left St Hugo of Grenoble in the Refectory of the Carthusians *(Francisco Zurbarán, 1633). St Hugo helped establish their house in Grenoble, France.*

Over time, monastic orders lost their independent status and were required to obtain papal blessing and authorization.

LATE MEDIEVAL TIMES

During the Crusades, monastic rules of prayer and preaching were extended to include military and medical duties. The Knights Hospitaller of St John, which was founded in 1113, and the Knights Templar, established in 1119, both consisted of fighting men or soldier-nurses.

Above The monastery of Monte Cassino, originally established by St Benedict, had to be rebuilt after severe bombing by the Allies in WWII.

Other religious orders were established in the 13th century, which returned to the asceticism of the early Desert Fathers. They included the Franciscans, founded by St Francis of Assisi, the Dominicans of St Dominic, the Carmelites, and the Augustinian Hermits. These were all mendicant orders, relying on charity for survival. Although the monks were attached to a community, they functioned as individuals.

Nuns generally lived in their enclosed communities, isolated from the outside world. They followed the Rule of St Francis through St Clare, or that of the Dominicans or Benedictines.

COME THE REFORMATION

During and after the Reformation, orders developed to strengthen the faith. Priests concentrated on teaching, nursing, leading retreats or missions. Most famous were the Jesuits, a missionary order founded by Ignatius of Loyola in 1534.

The Reformation reinforced eremitical orders. The Capuchins evolved from the Franciscans in 1525, the Trappists from the Cistercians in 1664, and the Maurists from the Benedictines in 1621. The Discalced Carmelites developed from the rule of St Clare in 1593.

Below A 15th-century drawing of monks wearing the distinctive habits of their orders. The Carmelites wore white, the Franciscans brown or grey, the Benedictines black, and the Dominicans black and white.

KNIGHTS HOSPITALLER OF ST JOHN

For centuries, a nursing order ran a hospital in Jerusalem. Then, in the 1120s, Raymond du Puy turned the order into a military community known as the Knights Hospitaller of St John. Nursing was not abandoned, but during the Crusades, the monks became much-feared soldiers. Expelled from Jerusalem by the Turks in 1291, they went to Rhodes.

Later, in the 16th century, the order was forced to move to Malta, where it remained until 1798. In 1834, after demonstrating that they had left their military past behind them, the order was allowed to settle in Rome.

Above Order of St John of Jerusalem, a woodcut dating from the 14th century.

PATRON SAINTS OF NATIONS

NATIONS EVERYWHERE HAVE CHOSEN PATRON SAINTS AS SPECIAL
GUARDIANS OVER THEIR COUNTRY. IN TIMES OF NATIONAL PERIL,
COUNTRYMEN ASK THEIR SAINT TO PRAY TO GOD FOR THEM.

Above Saint Rose of Lima *(Carlo Dolci, 17th century).*

Albania – Mary
Algeria – Cyprian
Andorra – Our Lady of Meritxell
Argentina – Francis Solano
Armenia – Bartholomew
Australia – Francis Xavier
Austria – Leopold III, Rupert
Belgium – Joseph
Bolivia – Francis Solano
Borneo – Francis Xavier
Bosnia – James the Great
Brazil – Peter of Alcantara,
   Antony of Padua
Bulgaria – Cyril and Methodius
Canada – Anne, George, Joseph
Chile – Francis Solano
China – Francis Xavier
Colombia – Luis Bertran,
   Peter Claver
Corsica – Devota
Costa Rica – Mary
Crete – Titus
Croatia – Joseph
Cuba – Mary

Cyprus – Barnabas
Czech Republic – Wenceslas
Denmark – Anskar, Canute
Dominican Republic – Dominic
Ecuador – Mary
Egypt – Mark
El Salvador – Mary
England – George
Ethiopia – Frumentius
Finland – Henry of Finland
France – Denys of Paris, Joan of
   Arc, Theresa of Lisieux
Georgia – George
Germany – Boniface
Gibraltar – Bernard of Clairvaux
Gozo – George
Greece – Nicholas of Myra, Paul
Guatemala – James the Great
Haiti – Mary
Honduras – Mary
Hungary – Stephen of Hungary
Iceland – Thorlac of Skalholt
India – Rose of Lima, Thomas
Indonesia – Mary
Iran – Maruthas
Ireland – Brigid, Patrick
Italy – Catherine of Siena, Francis
   of Assisi

Below Detail from a 13th-century mosaic showing scenes from the life of St Mark.

Jamaica – Mary
Japan – Francis Xavier, Peter
Jordan – John the Baptist
Korea – Joseph
Kosovo – Methodius
Lithuania – Casimir of Poland
Luxembourg – Willibrord
Macedonia – Clement of Okhrida
Madagascar – Vincent de Paul
Malta – George, Paul
Mexico – Our Lady of Guadalupe,
   Joseph
Monaco – Devota
Montenegro – George
Moravia – Wenceslas
Netherlands – Willibrord
New Zealand – Francis Xavier
Nicaragua – James the Great
Nigeria – Patrick
Norway – Olaf, Magnus
Oceania – Peter Chanel
Pakistan – Francis Xavier, Thomas
Palestine – George
Panama – Mary
Papua New Guinea – Archangel
   Michael
Paraguay – Francis Solano
Peru – Francis Solano, Rose of Lima

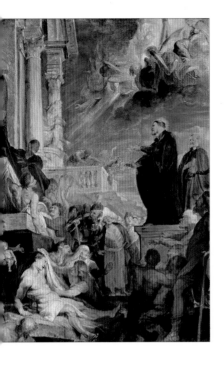

Far Left St Francis Xavier Blessing the Sick *(Rubens, 17th century).*

Left Nicetas *(Giovanni Antonio Guardi, 18th century).*

MARY, THE BLESSED VIRGIN

Many nations around the world have adopted Mary, mother of Jesus, as their patron, often in addition to other saints. In this feature she is listed only beside those states where she is sole patron.

Mary, the Blessed Virgin, is believed to appear in symbolic and visionary form at times of national crisis. The Philippine navy, for example, was convinced Mary hovered over their ships and helped them to repulse the enemy.

Another example comes from Albania. Catholics believe a canvas painting of the Virgin, lodged on a cliff, prevented bombs in World War II falling on their land.

Philippines – Rose of Lima
Poland – Stanislaus of Cracow, Casimir of Poland
Portugal – Antony of Padua, Francis Borgia
Puerto Rico – Mary
Romania – Cyril and Methodius, Nicetas
Russia – Nicholas of Myra, Andrew, Vladimir
Sardinia – Maurice
Scotland – Andrew, Margaret of Scotland
Serbia – Sava of Serbia
Sicily – Andrew Avellino
Slovakia – John of Nepomuk
Slovenia – Virgilius
South Africa – Mary
Spain – James the Great
Sri Lanka – Thomas
Sudan – Josephine Bakhita
Sweden – Bridget of Sweden, Eric of Sweden
Switzerland – Gall, Nicholas of Flue
Syria – Barbara
Tanzania – Mary
Tunisia – Mary
Turkey – John the Evangelist, John Chrysostom
Uganda – Mary
Ukraine – Josaphat
USA – Mary

Below Stained-glass window depicting St Andrew from the church of St Neot in Cornwall (16th century).

Uruguay – James the Less
Venezuela – Mary
Vietnam – Joseph
Wales – David
West Indies – Rose of Lima
Zaire – Mary

Above Enthroned Madonna with Child, Angels and Saints *(Lorenzetti, c.1340).*

FOURTEEN HOLY HELPERS

IN THE 14TH CENTURY, THE BLACK DEATH STRUCK TERROR IN THE POPULATIONS OF EUROPE. AS A SOURCE OF RELIEF TO ROMAN CATHOLIC VICTIMS, THE POPE SET UP A SPECIAL GROUP OF SAINTS.

A magnificent chapel was built in the 18th century to house the statues of the Fourteen Holy Helpers. Within its Baroque interior, massed in a circle around the altar, stand 14 figures, each representing a saint. The Vierzehnheiligen Sanctuary was built in Germany in veneration of these saints, who were first grouped together during the Black Death of the 14th century.

IMMORTAL PERIL

This disease was terrifying in its symptoms and caused rapid death. People were dying before they received the last rites.

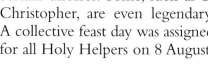

"Remember the dangers that surround us in this vale of tears, and intercede for us in all our needs and adversities. Amen"

A PRAYER OF INVOCATION TO THE FOURTEEN HOLY HELPERS

This both saddened and frightened the faithful, who believed that without receiving this sacrament, they would forego the essential final step on the journey to heaven. To compensate in some measure for the lack of a priest available to serve the last rites, sufferers could call upon any one of these specified saints to intercede on their behalf for the absolution of their sins.

Some of the Helpers are martyrs, others are associated with certain diseases. Some, such as St Christopher, are even legendary. A collective feast day was assigned for all Holy Helpers on 8 August.

MEANING THROUGH ART

As well as the statues in the sanctuary in Germany, there are many other representations of the Fourteen Holy Helpers, particularly from the 14th and 15th centuries.

Images of the figures were usually placed near church altars, often with Mary, the Blessed Virgin, cradling the Baby Jesus, or with St Christopher carrying the Christ Child on his shoulders.

Left St Roch Praying to the Virgin for an End to the Plague *(Jacques-Louis David, 1780).*

Above View of the Town Hall of Marseilles During the Plague of 1720 *(Michel Serre, 18th century).*

Paintings and sculptures often represent these saints as distorted, or holding awkward positions to indicate the symptoms they are believed to cure. Clothes or an animal companion might give a symbolic meaning or denote their traditional significance.

Indeed, some paintings are so grotesque in their depictions of diseases and suffering that the artists seem intent on bringing home the full horror of the Black Death to the viewer.

CULTUS IN EUROPE

For centuries, these images attracted large crowds. The cultus was strong in Germany, Hungary

THE PROTECTORS

- **Acacius** and **Denys of Paris** are called upon for headaches.
- **Barbara** intercedes for fevers and sudden death.
- **George** and **Pantaleon** protect domestic animals.
- **Blaise** guards against sore throats.
- **Catherine of Alexandria** and **Christopher** are patrons of sudden death.
- **Cyricus** helps to ward off temptation.
- **Margaret of Antioch** aids women in childbirth.
- **Vitus** prevents epilepsy.
- **Erasmus** is associated with intestinal troubles.
- **Eustace** helps out in difficult situations.
- **Giles** is invoked by lepers, the physically handicapped, and nursing mothers.

and Scandinavia. But it never commanded much of a following in Italy, France or England.

The numbers of pilgrims decreased after the Reformation. Now this group of saints is relatively obscure to most Roman Catholic worshippers.

Above Martyrdom of St Erasmus *(Nicolas Poussin, 1629).*

The list of saints is generally stable, but substitutions were made in some regions or cities where the veneration of particular saints was strong. The Holy Helpers were invoked to guard against specific illnesses – and these included diseases suffered by animals as well as humans.

THE BLACK DEATH

The origin of this plague remains a mystery. It was a virulent epidemic that swept across Europe in 1348. It caused rapid putrefaction of the sufferer's body, which turned black before death occurred. In Europe, 25 million died, including one-third of the English population. The numbers of victims in Asia and North Africa are unknown.

There were other outbreaks of plague in Europe but none so devastating as the Black Death. Its cause has been attributed variously to unknown substances, germs introduced by sailors, or a predominance of rats. The lack of hygiene found in medieval cities was a major factor.

Above Black Death at Tournai *(Gilles Le Muisit, 1349).*

WARRIOR SAINTS

WHETHER SOLDIERS OF WAR OR FOR PEACE, MANY MEN AND WOMEN SINCE THE BIRTH OF CHRISTIANITY HAVE BEEN CANONIZED FOR DEFENDING THEIR FAITH AND GOING INTO BATTLE.

Throughout history, soldiers have often claimed that the saints have aided and protected them in battle. Many warriors have converted to Christianity and died for their faith, or fought bloody wars to protect their right to worship their God. There are others whose inspiration came from Christ himself and who took to the path of peace.

HEAVENLY INSPIRATION

The archangel Michael, "captain of the heavenly host" and protector of Christian soldiers, has often appeared above battlefields or kept company with troops in combat. Joan of Arc identified him as helping spur her into battle.

In their long battle against Moorish invasion, the Spanish frequently called upon the apostle St James the Great, patron saint of Spain. After the miraculous victory at the Battle of Clavijo (AD 844), the soldiers claimed that James had appeared in their midst in full armour, sword in one hand and banner in the other, riding a white charger.

SOLDIER SAINTS

Since the days of the Roman Empire, there have been military men who have rejected their earthly masters and pledged to serve only Christ.

Known in the Eastern Orthodox Church as the "Great Martyr", St Demetrius was much admired as a warrior saint. He was a soldier in the Roman army in the early 4th century, who converted to Christianity and was subsequently put to death.

Above St Maurice, fresco detail (artist unknown, 15th century).

A great soldier saint and inspiration to warriors and crusaders, St George is always depicted as a knight in armour. Although most of what we know is legendary, he is venerated throughout the Christian world. St George is thought to have been martyred at Lydda in Palestine around AD 303.

St Theodore, known as "the recruit", was a young Roman soldier. After his conversion to Christianity he refused to join his comrades in the worship of pagan gods. Tradition says that he also set fire to a pagan temple. He was martyred in the 4th century at Pontus (part of modern Turkey).

During birthday celebrations for the Roman emperors Diocletian and Maximian, a centurion named Marcellus threw off his soldier's belt crying, "I am a soldier of Christ, the eternal king, and from now I cease to serve you." Other Roman soldiers who

Left Camillus of Lellis rescues hospital patients during the flooding of the Tiber in 1598 (Pierre Subleyras, 1745).

converted expressed the same anti-military sentiments, such as St Julius who chose to die by the sword rather than serve a master on earth.

There are also great leaders who are much venerated because they were soldiers in service of Christ. St Stephen of Hungary, a skilled military strategist, set out to conquer the pagans in his country and force them to convert to the Christian faith. St Vladimir of Kiev is revered throughout Orthodox Russia as the man who brought Christianity to his country, although initially he used the army to impose the new faith.

PEACEFUL PATH

Some soldier converts came to realize that the Christian life was not compatible with violence.

Martin of Tours, a young officer in the Roman army, asked for a discharge after his conversion. He announced, "I am Christ's soldier; I am not allowed to fight."

Left Alexander Nevski (artist unknown, 1855).

Much later, in the 16th century, St Camillus of Lellis was a mercenary or "soldier of fortune" who began nursing the sick and injured after his conversion. He is credited with organizing the first field ambulance unit, going into the battlefield to care for the wounded. St John of God was another mercenary whose conversion made him seek peace. He also turned to nursing and founded the Brothers Hospitallers.

During the Spanish Civil War of 1936–39, thousands of Christians fought for a country that was guided by the faith against their fellow citizens who wanted a secular regime. Hundreds of the Catholics who died were beatified by Pope John Paul II and are known as the Martyrs of the Spanish Civil War.

Below St Demetrius (Serbian icon, 18th century).

THE CRUSADES

In the Middle Ages, European Christian countries mounted military campaigns to oust the Muslims from Jerusalem and give support to Christians isolated in the East.

There were eight Crusades in all, lasting from 1095 to 1272 and ending with the Muslims still in control. Vast sums of money and huge numbers of men were involved. The journey to the Holy Land involved travelling great distances and was often disrupted by battles on land and sea. The Crusaders often fought while weak with hunger and ravaged by disease.

The Crusaders believed they had God on their side and often experienced heavenly visions. They adopted St George and St Demetrius as patron saints after they appeared above the demoralized soldiers and led them to victory against the Saracens at the Siege of Antioch (1097–98).

King Louis IX of France led two disastrous crusades in 1248 and 1270. Although he was not victorious, he was venerated for his zeal in fighting for the Holy Land.

Left The archangel Michael (Greek, c.14th century).

Above Manuscript illumination showing soldiers departing for the Crusades (c.1240–84).

THE SAINTS IN ART

PAINTINGS OF THE SAINTS INSPIRED BELIEVERS TO FEEL THAT, IN CONTEMPLATING HOLY IMAGES, THEY WOULD DRAW CLOSER TO GOD. PERSONAL ATTRIBUTES WERE ADDED TO IDENTIFY THE SAINTS.

Gregory the Great observed that paintings do for the illiterate what texts do for readers. There can be little doubt that the medieval faithful, most of whom could not read, were uplifted by illustrations of the saints' lives.

Despite the passing of centuries, believers who gazed upon these images were not dismayed by various artistic developments. Changes to the style of clothing worn by the saints or altered settings tended to cause no discomfort among the faithful. Neither did the portrayal of particular saints with different faces in successive paintings.

Above The Martyrdom of St Catherine of Alexandria *(Lucas Cranach the Elder, 1506).*

SYMBOLS OF IDENTITY

From early in the history of Christian art, a convention arose to identify saints through symbols. These emblems served to clarify the narrative being told, and to identify the characters.

Mary, the Blessed Virgin, and infant Jesus are instantly recognizable. Likewise, Mary holding her dead son, a scene known as the Pietà, is universally understood, as is the image of the crucifix, representing the crucified Christ.

But other characters needed their individual code of identity in order to be recognized, since no one knew what the saints looked like. To modern eyes, medieval and Renaissance Christian paintings can look quaint, even bizarre.

Doves emanate rays of light, lions lie meekly on cathedral floors, and a stag might display a crucifix within its antlers. Angels have blue duck-feathered wings, and men stand, pierced by arrows or even holding their own heads. For some 1,700 years, these unlikely elements possessed a beautiful logic, easily understood by all Christians, from the bogs of Ireland to the deserts of Syria.

Above St Lucy with her eyes on a plate (Umbrian School, c.1550).

LIONS TO ALABASTER

The medieval faithful knew the scholarly man with the lion was St Jerome. Likewise, the man with an arrow was Sebastian, who by tradition was shot in this manner.

The shepherdess, St Margaret of Antioch, carried a staff and was shown with a dragon because she escaped from such a beast. St James the Great had a seashell and pilgrim's staff near him. The shell

Below St Jerome in the Desert (Pietro Perugino, c.1499–1502).

> "The work shines nobly,
> but the work which shines nobly should clear minds,
> so that they may travel through the true lights
>   to the true light
> where Christ is the true door."
>
> ABBOT SUGER (c.1081–1151)

indicated his body was found in a drifting boat, the staff that he was a journeying evangelist.

All Christendom recognized Mary Magdalene because a jar of ointment and loosened hair marked her apart. With oil of alabaster she anointed Christ's feet before drying them with her hair.

ART AS IDOLATRY

The Church regarded artistic representations as an expression of the holiness of the saints. In the

Below A fresco showing the popular subject of St Luke painting the Madonna (Andrea Delitio, 1477).

Orthodox Church, they were used to concentrate the mind during meditation. But these artistic works aroused anxiety during the Reformation.

Protestant leaders forbade the erection of any kind of image in religious buildings. Images were regarded as idolatrous on the ground that the Old Testament forbids worship before idols.

Paintings, shrines and statues of saints were cleared away and frescoes were concealed behind a covering of wall paint. These zealous reformers even showed hostility toward music. The Roman Catholic Church uses

music for worship. The Eastern Orthodox Church retains a sung liturgy so revered it has remained unaltered to this day.

The reformer John Calvin declared that music had no place in a church. The less stern Martin Luther, on the other hand, composed his own church hymns.

SAINTLY ARTISTS

There are saints who were artists, the first being the Apostle Luke, reported to have made studies of Mary, the Blessed Virgin. Perhaps the greatest painter is Fra Angelico whose spiritual paintings are famous, but the drawings and music of Hildegard of Bingen also carry a mystical quality.

Musicians and poets can be found in the company of saints. It is assumed Gregory the Great was a musician – one reason for this assumption is that the Gregorian Chants bear his name.

There are contemporary reports that describe Nicetas of Remesiana as a poet and composer who wrote the beautiful Latin hymn, *Te Deum*. He used music as a form of preaching.

Above Manuscript illumination from Cantigas de Santa Maria (Alphonse Le Sage, 13th century).

ROYAL SAINTS

MANY MONARCHS ARE VENERATED FOR THEIR BRAVE DEFENCE OF
CHRISTIANITY. SOME GAVE THEIR LIVES FOR THAT CAUSE; OTHERS
RULED WITH ESPECIAL WISDOM AND BENEVOLENCE.

It may be difficult to reconcile the virtuous qualities of saint-hood with the characteristics of the rich and mighty, but many saints were, in fact, also powerful monarchs. In their privileged positions, these holy men and women ruled with great fortitude, promoting Christianity through example and sacrifice.

Left St Cunegund, empress and wife of Henry II, holding the model of a church (the Master of Messkirch, c.1530–38).

Right Edward the Confessor in stained glass from Canterbury, England (15th century).

WARRIOR SAINTS
Many kings have been involved in warfare, protecting their borders and Christianity on behalf of their countrymen. Some, including Vladimir and Alexander Nevski, were soldiers. These early rulers of Russia used arms to quell invaders but proved righteous monarchs.

Henry II, another militant man, went to war to establish the borders of Germany and became emperor in 1014. After this, he turned to his religion and prayer, built monasteries, and promoted welfare for the poor. He was said to be so pious that his marriage was never consummated. Henry II was canonized in 1146, while his wife Cunegund was canonized in 1200.

Other saintly warrior kings include Stephen of Hungary, who limited the power of the nobles, reduced tribal tensions and installed a judicial system. Stephen made Hungary a Christian country, and was a heroic leader.

SPREADING THE FAITH
As Christianity began to take root in Europe, monarchs played a vital role in imparting the faith to their subjects. English kings, such as Ethelbert of Kent and Oswald, were pioneers of the faith and venerated for encouraging the

first Christian missions. Edward the Confessor was known for his visions and miraculous cures of the ill. He devoted much of his time to the establishment of the Church and the monasteries in England and was loved for his kind and fair rule.

Norway's patron saint, King Olaf, established the Christian faith among his people and, after

"Dear son, if you come to reign, do that which befits a king, that is, be so just as to deviate in nothing from justice, whatever may befall you."

ST LOUIS, KING OF FRANCE

Above A statue of Stephen of Hungary near the Freedom Bridge in Budapest, Hungary.

his death in battle, was credited with miracles and a healing spring that began to flow from his grave.

MARTYRED MONARCHS

Several Christian monarchs have been martyred for their faith. One was the English boy king, Edward the Martyr, who was killed in AD 979 in a power struggle for the throne. Another, Edmund of Abingdon, was cruelly murdered by Viking invaders when he refused to deny his faith.

Two Scandinavian kings, Canute of Denmark and Eric of Sweden, also gave their lives for their Christian beliefs. Canute's murder at an altar was followed by many miracles and wonders. Sweden became a Christian country under Eric, but he was tortured and beheaded by attacking soldiers. These Scandinavian kings had large cultuses until the Reformation, when the Protestant movement began to overwhelm the Roman Catholic Church in northern Europe.

QUEENLY SAINTS

By the 11th century, the Scots had a pious queen. Margaret of Scotland was recognized for both her devotion to her family and her deep faith, as witnessed by her charitable work for the poor and for prisoners.

Elizabeth of Portugal was married to King Denis of Portugal. He was a violent man, but she converted him to the faith. She brought comfort and aid to orphans and "fallen women", and founded hospitals. Pilgrims and the very poor turned to her for hospitality and care.

Her distant relative, after whom she was named, Elizabeth of Hungary, likewise established hospitals, as well as founding the first orphanage in central Europe. The final part of her life was austere, poverty-stricken and devoted to prayer and charity. Her relics at the church of St Elizabeth at Marburg drew hordes of pilgrims until, in 1539, the Lutheran Philip of Hesse removed them and hid them in an unknown site.

Right A portrait of St Vladimir (anonymous Russian artist, 1905).

Although many later monarchs continued to support the Catholic Church and to exercise their rule with Christian values, few European kings or queens were canonized after the Reformation.

KING LOUIS IX OF FRANCE

Louis IX took up arms for his faith, but he dedicated much of his life to spiritual causes. His subjects knew him as a man who was severe in his habits, devoting long hours to prayer. He built monasteries and a hospital for the poor. He was also admired for his efforts to show justice, even though his courtiers sometimes thwarted his good intentions. His courage in fighting for Christendom aroused great respect and he led two crusades, meeting his death at Tunis in 1270. During this last expedition, Louis tried to reconcile the Greeks to the Church of Rome.

Above King Louis IX of France (St Louis) embarking on his first Crusade in 1248 (manuscript illumination, c.1325).

SAINTLY POPES

THE FIRST POPES ARE VENERATED AS MARTYRS OF THE FAITH, BUT MANY OTHERS ARE REVERED FOR THE WISDOM, STRENGTH AND SPIRITUAL LEADERSHIP THEY DEMONSTRATED IN OFFICE.

The role of the papacy has often been fraught with spiritual and political strife. When Christianity was just beginning to be established, during persecution by the Roman Empire, a number of early popes were martyred for their faith. Later, popes struggled to unite the Church, which was being damaged by warring factions and corruption. Many of these holy men have been canonized in recognition of their faithfulness and spiritual leadership.

THE MARTYRS

One of the first popes, Clement I, who died around AD 100, was a contemporary of Sts Peter and Paul. He was credited with miraculous powers, and some of his writings are extant, revealing him as a thoughtful theologian. His Epistle to the Corinthians is significant because it marks the first

> "When the work of God is finished, let all go out with the deepest silence, and let reverence be shown to God."
>
> FROM THE RULE OF ST BENEDICT

time a bishop of Rome intervened in the business of another Church. Clement I was martyred by having an anchor tied to his neck and being pushed into the sea. Allegedly, angels built him a tomb on the seabed, and this could be seen when the sea was at low tide.

Pope Callistus was born a slave and rebelled against Roman law by promoting marriage between freeborn Christians and slaves. Kind and forgiving, he was thrown

Above A fresco of Leo the Great (Italian School, 8th century AD).

down a well and drowned in AD 222. Pope Cornelius was likewise resented for his policy of forgiveness to those who truly repented their sins. His attitude caused a split among churchmen, and the Romans beheaded him.

Sixtus II, who became pope in AD 257, was killed by the sword one year after he took office.

LEADERS OF THE FAITH

One of the most influential early popes was Leo the Great. During his reign, he freed Rome from the barbarians and healed a Church fractured by war and the spread of pagan beliefs. Both the people and the clergy needed clarification on Christian dogma. In a letter to the Council of Chalcedon, Leo explained that Jesus Christ is one person, in whom the divine and the human are united, but not mixed. This became a fundamental teaching of the Church.

Left Coronation of Pope Celestine V in August 1294 (French School, 16th century).

The Church continued to strengthen under the rule of Pope Gregory the Great, an austere, devout man, who succeeded in establishing the primacy of Rome against claims from the Eastern Orthodox Church. He developed the Church liturgy and mounted a successful mission to England.

Gregory II, too, was an energetic apostle. He instigated reforms in the clergy, built churches and sustained the Church's authority against secular power. The monastery at Monte Cassino was revived under his care, and he built another in Rome, St Paul's-outside-the-Walls.

DIVISION AND REFORM

The problems between the Eastern and Western branches of the Church became urgent during the office of Pope Leo IX (1002–54). Under his rule, the Church increased its independence from secular authority, and he sent legates to confer with Michael Cerularius, Patriarch of Constantinople. Leo died before the schism between the East and West had widened into total separation. Leo was a holy man, and many miracles were attributed to him after his death.

Pope Gregory VII continued his predecessors' reformation of the Church and alienated many powerful people in the process. He was determined to stop the practice of laymen appointing officers of the Church, because these laymen were often the rich

Left Gregory the Great dictating a manuscript (illuminated manuscript, 9th century).

and powerful, who used the clergy to extend their secular ambitions. The German Emperor Henry IV was infuriated by this reform and tried to depose Gregory, though he later famously repented by standing at the palace gates for three days in the snow.

Peter Celestine (or Celestine V) founded the Celestine Order, but was an unwilling and unworldly pope. He abdicated his office but was still canonized for his devout nature in 1313.

In the 16th century, while the Church was still reeling from the Reformation, Pope Pius V provided vigorous leadership. A key figure in the Counter-Reformation, he helped rid the Church of heresy and corruption, controlled excessive spending by the bishops, and reformed the liturgy, making the words and rituals accessible to ordinary worshippers.

Indeed, throughout the centuries, the popes who have attained sainthood are often men who have brought remarkable devotion and wise leadership to the papal office.

Left St Peter's Basilica and Square, Rome, as depicted in the 18th century.

POPE PIUS X

Pope Pius X wanted "to renew all things in Christ". He opened the Church and her liturgy to ordinary people, encouraged daily attendance at Mass and welcomed children to partake of the Holy Eucharist. Church music was modernized, and on Sundays, Pius X would deliver a short sermon in a Vatican courtyard, which anyone was welcome to attend. He faced problems with the French state, and was forced to sacrifice Church property in exchange for freedom from secular control. He also restated the Christian doctrine against what he saw as heretical interpretations, in what he termed the "Modernist" crisis. After his death in 1914, a cultus came quickly into being.

Above Pope Pius X (c.1905).

THE MARTYRS OF CHINA

THESE MARTYRS REPRESENT THOUSANDS OF CHRISTIANS WHO WERE TORTURED AND KILLED FOR THEIR CHRISTIAN FAITH IN CHINA OVER A PERIOD OF MORE THAN 400 YEARS.

The history of Christianity in China is a turbulent one that has involved much persecution. The first contact Chinese people had with Christianity was from the Nestorian heresy, which spread East, reaching China by the early 6th century AD.

Later, relative stability, brought by the Mongol expansion in Asia during the 13th and 14th centuries, opened up routes between the East and West and led to direct contact being established between China and Europe. Among those taking advantage of this new connection to the East were missionaries, who were eager to spread the Christian message.

EARLY CHINESE MISSIONS
The first Roman Catholic mission to China was led by Bishop John of Montecorvino (1246–1328), who established friendly relations with the Yuan dynasty.

Unfortunately, later missionaries were not so well received. The Yuan dynasty fell in 1368, and later regimes showed violent hos-

tility to foreigners and foreign religions. Many missionaries to China never returned. Some were defeated by the harsh conditions of travel. One such was Francis Xavier, who died in 1551 soon after being refused entry to the country. Others were deliberately targeted by the ruling powers in China. This was the destiny of Francisco Fernandez de Capillas, a Dominican, who led a mission to Fujian and was beheaded during the early Ching dynasty in 1648.

Above Father Adam Schall von Bell (1591–1666) was a German Jesuit missionary to China (German School, 17th century).

Above St Jean-Gabriel Perboyre, martyred in China in 1840 (François Constant Petit, 19th century).

THE CHING DYNASTY
The Ching dynasty was particularly anti-Christian, and officials of the regime hounded Christians in China for 400 years. Among the victims were Spanish Dominican missionary Pedro Sanz, who was murdered in 1747, and Francis Regis Clet of St Vincent de Paul, who died in 1820.

Despite the killings of foreign missionaries and thousands of Chinese converts, the faith took root. Early in the 20th century, the Rev. Fang Ho collected the relics of these early Chinese martyrs and translated them to Taipei in Taiwan where they rest in the Chinese Blessed Martyrs Church in Peng Chiao.

Archives from the 19th century record details of some of the martyrs of that period. These names

Left A figure of St Paul inside St Paul's Church in Macau, China.

"Almighty God, we give you thanks for choosing many Chinese faithful to witness for Christ by giving up their lives... We also pray that we may follow the example of these Chinese by remaining strong in faith, hope and love..."

EXCERPT FROM PRAYER TO THE CHINESE MARTYRS

are included among the 120 Martyrs of China. The latter were chosen to represent the thousands of anonymous victims of religious persecution. First among them is Peter Wu Guosheng, who died in 1814. Another is Agnes Cao Guiying, an account of whose torture and martyrdom in 1856 can be found in Chinese court records. She was kept in a cage so small she could not move her limbs to sit, and died in captivity.

Other known martyrs come from records dated during 1900, at the time of the Boxer Rebellion, when the Chinese rose up against everything perceived as foreign. European and Chinese Christians, nuns and priests, women and children were brutally murdered for their faith. Among them were Mary Guo-Li, who died alongside her four grandchildren and two daughters-in-law. All were beheaded on 7 July 1900. Lang-Yang and her seven-year-old son, Paolo, were stabbed and burnt a few days later. More than 30 men and women were dragged from their cathedral in Taiyuan, Shanxi Province. They were given time to take Mass and pray before they were beheaded in a mass execution on 9 July 1900. They, too, are named among the Martyrs of China.

Above Funeral of St Jean-Louis Bonnard at the seminary of Nam-Dinh (artist unknown, 19th century).

COMMUNISM

The Ching dynasty was toppled in 1907, and after years of war, the Communists took power. Their persecution of Christians was as fierce as that of the previous regime. Churches were burnt, unknown thousands of Christians martyred, and it seemed that the faith had finally been eradicated. Even the ownership of a Bible could lead to imprisonment or execution. However, the faithful did not abandon their beliefs. Instead, they met in secret, risking harsh punishment.

Pope John Paul II proclaimed the 120 Blessed Martyrs of China as saints in 2000. Among them are 33 foreign missionaries and 87 Chinese, including bishops, priests, nuns, friars and 76 lay people. In 2007, the Chinese government gave the Roman Catholic Church permission to build a church, the first in more than 70 years. Christianity is now officially recognized in China and public worship is permitted in churches and cathedrals. No longer persecuted, 22 million Chinese people – Protestants and Catholics – have publicly proclaimed their faith.

HYACINTH CASTANEDA

Hyacinth Castaneda was born in Setaro, Spain, but longed to spread the message of Christianity outside Europe. He travelled across the Atlantic, suffering from infection and seasickness, before walking across Mexico to reach the Pacific coast. From there, he travelled to the Philippines, where he was ordained, then took a boat to China. From his base in Fulcien, he started preaching and converted many people. The authorities arrested and imprisoned him in what is now Vietnam. He was held for three years, with fellow prisoner Vincent Liem and was branded and tortured. He was beheaded in 1773. He is listed among the Martyrs of Vietnam.

Below Missionaries to China were martyred in various ways: some were beheaded, others garrotted and some were burnt alive (Indo-Chinese School, 19th century).

INCORRUPTIBLES

ALL SAINTS ARE REVERED FOR THE WONDROUS ACTS, AND OFTEN MIRACLES, THEY PERFORM WHEN THEY ARE LIVING, BUT SOME SHOW EXTRAORDINARY PHYSICAL QUALITIES EVEN AFTER THEIR DEATH.

Above A portrait of Rita of Cascia in the church of Santa Maria del Giglio, Venice (19th century).

The words "incorrupt" and "incorruptible" are used by the Catholic Church to describe bodies that do not decompose after death. The body is considered incorrupt only if no preservation techniques, such as embalming, have been used, and it is not uncommon for the body's lack of decomposition to be accompanied by a sweet smell. The discovery of an incorrupt corpse is generally made by chance, and when the body of a holy person is found intact, it is traditionally taken as a sign of sainthood.

Alongside other miraculous phenomena associated with saints, including stigmata and the healing of the sick, the survival of a saint's corpse seems to defy any scientific explanation, and many Catholic Christians believe the holiness and piety of an incorruptible saint to be the cause of divine preservation.

EARLY INCORRUPTIBLES

A very early example of an incorruptible is the 3rd-century saint, Cecilia. When her tomb was opened in 1599, a thousand years after she was buried, her corpse showed no signs of corruption. Sadly, on exposure to the air, it quickly turned to dust.

Left A portrait of Bernadette of Lourdes (19th century).

There was frequent correspondence between Rome and the English clergy after the death of Edward the Confessor in 1066. A cultus grew around this king, and the campaign to have him canonized was strengthened when his body was found to be incorrupt in 1102. Monks from Westminster made enquiries and in 1161, Pope Innocent III finally agreed with their findings and advised that the saint's relics be translated to Westminster Abbey. In 1163, a procession carried the incorrupt body to its final resting place.

THE BLOOD OF ST JANUARIUS

St Januarius, who was martyred in AD 305, is the patron saint of Naples, and his presence is believed to protect the port from harm. Twice every year – on 19 September and on the Saturday before the first Sunday in May – a solemn procession, led by representatives of the Church, progresses through the city displaying a vial of St Januarius's blood, which liquefies and bubbles in just the same way as fresh blood. Believers fear a calamity would hit Naples if the blood failed to liquefy. Other saints whose blood was said to show this quality include Pantaleon, Stephen and John the Baptist.

Right Cardinal Crescenzio Sepe, Archbishop of Naples, looks at the glass vial holding the blood of St Januarius during the Feast of San Gennaro in 2006.

Above The incorrupt body of Catherine Labouré, kept at 140 rue du Bac in Paris, France.

Above The incorrupt body of Jean-Baptiste Vianney is kept in the Basilica at Ars, France.

St Rita of Cascia (1377–1447) is another incorruptible, whose face, hands and feet survive along with much of her skeleton. Her remains are on display in the Basilica of St Rita in Cascia, Italy.

THE LAST 200 YEARS

The body of Jean-Baptiste Vianney also remained intact after his death in 1859. He won the admiration of his congregation for his faith and goodness. They were amazed, too, by his meagre diet of boiled potatoes, and his habit of sleeping for a mere two or three hours a night. His extraordinary qualities in life were extended in death when his body did not decompose.

Madeleine Sophie Barat was an energetic woman who travelled widely and devoted herself to the Christian education of children. The miraculous preservation of her body, which is kept in Jette in Belgium, reflects the strength and vitality that she always demonstrated in life.

Another holy woman whose body has proved incorrupt is Catherine Labouré. This modest

> We should show honour to the saints of God, as being members of Christ, the children and friends of God, and our intercessors. Therefore, in memory of them we ought to honour any relics of theirs in a fitting manner.
>
> ST THOMAS AQUINAS

nun, who is venerated as a mystic, was canonized in 1947. She died in 1876 and her body rests in the convent where she lived for nearly half a century, in the chapel at 140 rue du Bac, Paris.

An equally humble woman whose body survives without corruption is Bernadette of Lourdes, who saw visions of the Virgin and lived piously as a nun. After her death in 1879, her corpse was removed three times from its resting place to undergo scientific examination. It now resides in a glass case in the convent at Nevers where visitors can marvel at its preserved state. Doctor Comte who examined St Bernadette's corpse in 1925 wrote, "…the body does not seem to have putrefied, nor has any decomposition of the body set in, although this would be expected and normal after such a long period in a vault hollowed out of the earth".

Right The incorrupt body of St Rita of Cascia is carried around Rome during a celebration on her feast day.

HOUSES OF GOD

MEDIEVAL CHURCHES WERE DESIGNED TO CAST THE MIND TOWARD
HEAVEN AND INSPIRE AWE. MODERN CHURCHES TEND TO BE MORE
SIMPLE AND INTIMATE TO HELP THE VISITOR FEEL CLOSER TO GOD.

Above The royal portal on the west
front of Notre-Dame Cathedral in
Chartres, France (c.1145).

As Christianity spread across
the Middle East and Europe,
so churches were built to provide
places of worship for believers. In
small towns and villages, these
buildings became the centre of
community life.

The church was the house of
God, and as such, money, time and
talent came to be lavished on
great cathedrals and grand
churches. The faithful entered
these wondrous buildings and
were filled with awe and reverence. Statues and paintings inside
confirmed the reality of the saints,
and Christians were convinced
that, in these surroundings, their
prayers would fly to heaven,
where the saints were listening.

THE GOTHIC STYLE

The medieval period saw the
building of churches throughout
the Christian world on an
unprecedented scale. In the West,
the predominant architectural
style was Gothic.

The Gothic architects erected
structures of great grandeur to
express the majesty of God and
emphasize man's insignificance.
These cathedrals featured huge
flying buttresses, pointed arches,
rib vaults, and large windows.
Enormous doors opened into
interiors lit by the mysterious
glow of stained glass.

> "I am the eternal door:
> pass through me, faithful
> ones. I am the fountain
> of life: thirst for me more
> than wine."
>
> THE PORTAL OF
> THE CHURCH OF
> SANTA CRUZ DE LA
> SERÓS, SPAIN

Façades were laced with deco-
ration and statues of saints, and to
remind the faithful of hell, small
devilish gargoyles flew from the
buttresses or were carved into
pews. One of the finest examples
of the Gothic style is the 12th-
century Notre-Dame Cathedral
in Chartres, France.

The construction of Gothic
cathedrals often took centuries
to complete, so these buildings
frequently incorporate a range of
architectural and artistic styles.

Left The front façade of the Cathedral
of St Michel and St Gudule in
Brussels, Belgium.

Construction of the Cathedral of
St Michel and St Gudule in
Brussels, for example, commenced
in the early 13th century but the
work was not completed for
another 300 years. Cologne
Cathedral, which has the largest
façade of any church in the world,
was begun in 1248 and finished
600 years later. Much of the
stained glass in the cathedral is
from the 19th century.

A NEW DIRECTION

When Martin Luther criticized
the power and practices of the
Roman Catholic Church in
1517, he began a new era for the
church in northern Europe,
known as the Reformation.

During the Reformation and
in its aftermath, exterior carvings
and statues, and the splendid interiors, walls hung with paintings,
reliquaries gleaming with precious metals and jewels, and even
the shrines so carefully constructed for relics were destroyed by
Luther's Protestant supporters.

A new and austere style
emerged, and this mood prevails
in much modern northern
European church architecture.
Architects of Protestant churches

Left The dome of the Hagia Sophia in Istanbul, Turkey. This magnificent Byzantine building was the mother church of the Eastern Christians for 916 years before it was turned into a mosque by the Ottomans in 1453. It is now a museum.

no longer seek to replicate heaven; neither do they wish to inspire awe in visitors. Churches are usually designed to be informal, and space is meant to promote fellowship among believers and stress a sense of community. Altar tables and light fittings are simple, and roof levels may be flattened or given low curves more in sympathy with an earthly landscape.

SURVIVAL OF DECORATION

Despite the efforts of the reformers, most medieval churches survived the Reformation. Even after the destructive Civil War in England, hundreds of examples are still relatively intact.

Where the Roman Catholic Church survived, or was unaffected by, the Reformation – in Italy, Spain, Poland, and parts of France and Germany – church architecture remained centred upon the glorification of God with beauty.

In the Balkans, Greece and the Middle East, where the Eastern Orthodox Church prevails, many ancient religious buildings can still be found, although some of these became mosques after the Islamic conquest of the East and the rule of the Ottoman Empire from Istanbul (once Constantinople).

Below The interior of Cologne Cathedral in Germany.

STAINED GLASS WINDOWS

The origin of the stained glass window is unknown, but artists were working in this medium by 1100. Coloured sections of glass, cut to shape and held together by black lead strips, formed elaborate designs that depicted biblical stories and lives of the saints. By the 16th century, artists preferred to paint the glass, and by the 18th century, many windows had been removed. Superb examples of medieval glass can still be seen in their original setting, for example at Notre-Dame Cathedral in Chartres, France, and York Minster in England. Many stained glass windows are preserved in the world's great museums.

Above A stained glass window at Chartres Cathedral showing St Lubin, Bishop of Chartres in the 6th century (c.1200–10).

THE CULT OF MARY

MARY, THE BLESSED VIRGIN, IS HONOURED WORLDWIDE BY MILLIONS OF FAITHFUL FOR HER PURITY AS WELL AS FOR HER EXTRAORDINARY ROLE AS THE MOTHER OF GOD.

Devotion to Mary can be traced as far back as the 4th or 5th centuries AD, but the full doctrine has developed gradually. In the earliest days of the Church, Mary, the Blessed Virgin, was called Christokos, "Mother of Christ", but this caused some wrangling among theologians because it implied that Jesus was not divine. In the 6th century AD, they agreed on Theotokos, "Mother of God", and this more emphatic description of Mary confirmed her strong position in the faith as the mother of Jesus, the Son of God. Even the Protestant Church accepted her unique role as the virgin mother of Christ, but some Protestant sects have recently questioned this.

Above A statue of the crowned Virgin and Child in Siena, Italy.

"Grant we beseech Thee, O Lord God, unto us thy servants, that we may rejoice in continual health of mind and body; and, by the glorious intercession of Blessed Mary ever Virgin, may be delivered from present sadness, and enter into the joy of thine eternal gladness. Through Christ our Lord.

Amen."

FINAL WORDS OF THE LITANY OF LORETO

in its calendar. The day of the Assumption, 15 August, occasions great celebration as it is considered to be Mary's heavenly birthday.

THE GREATEST SAINT
Mary has long been perceived as chief among all the saints, mediating with Jesus on behalf of the world. For this reason, the faithful turn to her to resolve their most difficult problems.

In 1587, Pope Sixtus V sealed this view of Mary's role when he approved the Litany of Loreto. In

AN EXCEPTIONAL WOMAN
Christians who venerate Mary often call her the Immaculate Conception. This refers to the belief that her spirit was conceived free from original sin, untainted by the sins of Adam and Eve in the Garden of Eden. This has led some theologians to refer to her as the "new Eve".

Not only is Mary believed to be immune from original sin, but she was also a virgin when Jesus was born, hence the title given to her, the Blessed Virgin. Because she embodies

Left A West African wood carving of Madonna and child (20th century).

purity and perfect motherly love, she has always held a special place in the heart of believers. Augustine of Hippo, when discussing the nature of Mary, said, "After all, how do we know what abundance of grace was granted to her who had the merit to conceive and bring forth him who was unquestionably without sin?"

When Mary had completed her life on earth, it is believed that she was received into heaven as a complete being – body and soul together. This special event is key to both Roman Catholic and Eastern Orthodox belief, but the Anglican Church also includes it

Right Catholics seek blessings for their child from a statue of Mary in Hyderabad, India.

Left An Ethiopian icon triptych depicting the Virgin and child (18th–19th century).

Catholic homes, schools and institutions display the image of the Blessed Virgin and often create small shrine-like altars in veneration of her. No Catholic church is without a statue to Mary, the Blessed Virgin and the infant Jesus.

In modern times, Mary is firmly lodged in the Christian culture. She is a central figure in literature and popular idiom, and she is patron saint to a number of countries.

The principal Marian shrines attract huge numbers of pilgrims, millions visiting every year the sites of Lourdes in France, Guadalupe in Mexico, Fatima in Portugal, Walsingham in England and the House of Loreto in Italy.

this long prayer, believers call upon God to heed Mary, and the text uses her many titles.

WORLDWIDE INFLUENCE

The Eastern Orthodox Church has been untouched by debate about Mary's role. There, she has always had a profound significance and many Orthodox icons are devoted to the image of Mary as Mother with her Holy Infant.

In the Western Church, theologians have long debated her role, but since the 15th century, popular religion has developed a deep devotion to Mary. She represents motherhood and family life, one who understands the universal experiences of joy and pain. Those believers suffering tragedy

Right The famous La Pietà in St Peter's, Rome (Michelangelo, 1496).

meditate on the image of Mary with her dying son. The rosary is a set of prayers often recited by Christians who venerate Mary, the Blessed Virgin. A string of beads, also called a rosary, is used as an aide-mémoire for the correct order of the prayers.

SOME TITLES OF MARY

There are numerous titles for Mary, many used in the long prayer, the Litany of Loreto. Here are a few examples:

Advocate of Grace
Champion of God's People
Chosen Daughter of the Father
Gracious Lady
Handmaid of the Lord
Holy Mary
Holy Mother of God
Joy of Israel
Most Honoured of Virgins
Mother of Christ
Mother Mary
Our Lady
Perfect Disciple of Christ
Queen of All Saints
Queen of Apostles and Martyrs
Queen of Confessors and Virgins
Queen of Mercy
Queen of Peace
Splendour of the Church
The Blessed Virgin
The Immaculate Conception

PATRON SAINTS

EACH BELIEVER NURSES A PARTICULAR AFFECTION FOR ONE OR MORE SAINTS, AND TURNS TO THESE HOLY SOULS FOR HELP AND PROTECTION. EVERY ASPECT OF LIFE IS UNDER SAINTLY GUARDIANSHIP, WHETHER IT IS BABYHOOD, COURTSHIP, DOG BITES OR LOST POSSESSIONS.

Early Christians, believing the saints to be alive in heaven, found it logical to see them as patrons for mortals on earth.

Saints were thought to look after certain sectors of society, as well as support themes or activities with resonance in their personal story.

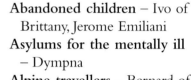

Above St Jerome Emiliani, the patron saint of lost children, with a young orphan boy (Giovanni Domenico Tiepolo, 1780).

Abandoned children – Ivo of Brittany, Jerome Emiliani

Asylums for the mentally ill – Dympna

Alpine travellers – Bernard of Montjoux

Babies – Holy Innocents, Maximus, Nicholas of Tolentino, Philip Zell

Beggars – Giles

Birds – Gall

Blind people – Thomas the Confessor, Cosmas and Damian, Archangel Raphael

Blood donors – Mary, the Blessed Virgin, Our Lady of the Thorns

Booksellers – John of God

Boys – Dominic Savio

Breastfeeding – Basilissa, Giles

Brides – Dorothy

Cemeteries – Michael, Anne

Childbirth – Margaret of Antioch, Raymund Nonnatus, Leonard of Noblac, Erasmus

Children, longing for – Rita of Cascia

Children, lost – Jerome Emiliani

Criminals – Dismas

Degree candidates – Joseph of Copertino

Dentists – Apollonia

Difficult situations – Eustace

Dog bites – Ubaldo

Left Ferdinand III ruled as a king in Spain in the 13th century (illuminated manuscript, c.1250). He is the patron of prisoners and the poor.

Doubters – Joseph (husband of Mary)
Drought – Genevieve
Emigrants – Frances Cabrini
Epilepsy – Dympna, Vitus
Falling – Venantius Fortunatus
Flying – Joseph of Copertino
Geese – Martin of Tours
Girls – Maria Goretti
Harvests – Antony of Padua
Heart patients – John of God
Hermits – Antony, Giles, Hilarion
Homeless – Benedict Joseph Labre
Horses – Eloi, Martin of Tours, Hippolytus
Hospitals – Camillus of Lellis, John of God
House hunting – Joseph (husband of Mary)
Housewives – Martha
Infertility – Rita of Cascia
Invalids – Roch
Journeys – Christopher, Nicholas of Bari, Archangel Raphael, Joseph (husband of Mary)
Kings – Edward the Confessor, Louis IX, Henry II
Knights – George, James the Greater
Learning – Catherine of Alexandria
Lost causes – Jude
Lost things – Antony of Padua
Lovers – Valentine
Married women – Monica
Marriage – John Francis Regis
Motherhood – Nicholas of Tolentino
Motorists – Christopher
Mountaineers – Bernard of Aosta
Music – Cecilia, Gregory the Great
Navigators – Brendan the Navigator, Erasmus, Nicholas of Myra
Old people – Teresa of Jesus Jornet y Ibars
Orphans – Ivo of Brittany, Jerome Emiliani
Paralysed – Osmund
Pets – Antony of Egypt
Pilgrims – Christopher, Nicholas of Myra
Poison sufferers – Benedict, John, Pirmin
Poor people – Antony of Padua, Ferdinand III

Pregnant women – Margaret of Antioch
Prisoners – Leonard of Noblac, Roch, Vincent de Paul, Ferdinand III of Castile
Rabies – Hubert, Ubaldo
Race relations – Martin de Porres, Peter Claver
Radio – Archangel Gabriel
Repentant prostitutes – Mary Magdalene, Mary of Egypt, Margaret of Cortona
Rheumatism sufferers – James the Great, Philip Neri
Restaurants – Martha
Retreats – Ignatius of Loyola
Shortsightedness – Clarus (abbot)
Shepherds – Cuthbert, Bernadette
Sleepwalkers – Dympna

Above St Giles, patron saint of beggars and cripples, was a hermit who probably lived in France in the 9th century (high altar of the Pacher School, c.1500).

Spas – John the Baptist
Stamp collectors – Archangel Gabriel
Television – Clare of Assisi
Teenage girls – Maria Goretti
Throat infections – Blaise
Toothache sufferers – Apollonia, Médard, Osmund, Cunibert of Cologne
Tourists – Francis Xavier
Unhappily married women – Wilgefortis, Rita of Cascia
Workers – Joseph (husband of Mary)
Youth – Aloysius Gonzaga

A·PERCITI·NAVIGIO·ALEX·ADRIA·T·RAD
RAVIT

VENERATED SAINTS

The first Christian saints were recognized soon after Christ's death over two thousand years ago and new names have been added ever since. This chapter features a selection of the most major and well known saints chronologically in order of their deaths. A strong historical sense emerges from studying these biographies, while changing cultural systems form a background to their stories.

Many saints are surrounded by myths of super-human strength and startling powers of endurance. The legends can be viewed as entertaining tales, yet they linger in the mind because these impossible acts are underwritten by a sincere faith. But, generally, the lives show the humanity of the saints; some were short-tempered, confused or bewildered, others had brilliant minds or a pious simplicity. We see kings becoming humble, peasant maids honoured for their integrity, and illiterates making an impact on the world theology. The difficulties and problems encountered in their lives mirror the political and social worlds they inhabited. The persecution of Christians during the Roman Empire is familiar to most, but perhaps less well known is the persecution of later times.

The company of saints is varied and complex, filled with eccentric personalities, but what is evident even in this small selection is that all are alike in their pious attachment to God.

Left Detail from a 13th-century mosaic showing scenes from the life of St Mark, the patron saint of Egypt.

Top St Francis Borgia (Francisco José de Goya y Lucientes, 1795).

MARY THE VIRGIN

MARY IS THE UNIVERSAL SYMBOL OF PURITY AND MOTHERHOOD. MANY
CHRISTIANS BELIEVE SHE WAS FREE OF SIN FROM THE MOMENT SHE WAS
CONCEIVED, A DOCTRINE KNOWN AS THE IMMACULATE CONCEPTION.

KEY FACTS
*Mother of the
Son of God*
DATES: *1st century BC*
BIRTH PLACE: *Unknown*
PATRON OF: *Motherhood,
virginity*
FEAST DAY: *15 August*
EMBLEM: *Blue robes, crown, lily*

The image of Mary, the Blessed Virgin, is instantly recognizable, whether as a mother with her child in her arms or with her dead son laid across her lap. Mary, in the role of the Holy Mother, represents feelings understood by everyone. No saint can match the mother of the Son of God.

EARLY LIFE
Little is known about Mary's early life. There are no dates for her birth or her death, and mention of her parents Anne and Joachim is only found in the apocryphal 2nd-century AD Gospel of James. The Bible states that she was descended from the family of the great Israelite king, David.

MOTHER OF CHRIST
It was the angel Gabriel who told Mary that she was to be the mother of Christ, an event known as the Annunciation. The angel said that the child would be the Son of God, not of a man. Mary accepted this with great faith and courage.

After the Nativity, Mary is mentioned only a few times in the gospels. Mary and Joseph took Jesus for his

Left A sculpture of Mary cradling the body of her dead son (I. Günther, 18th century). Artistic images of this moment are known as "the Pietà".

Left Mary and the baby Jesus are depicted as playful and loving in this stained glass from Eaton Bishop, England (14th century).

presentation at the Temple of Jerusalem. With Joseph and Jesus she fled to Egypt to save their child from slaughter by Herod's men. At the marriage feast at Canaan, Mary asked Jesus to intervene when the wine ran out. When Jesus hung dying on the cross, Mary kept vigil, and she was with the apostles at Pentecost. Nothing is known of Mary's death, but the Roman Catholic and Eastern Orthodox Churches hold that she was lifted body and soul into heaven.

MARY IN ART
During the early medieval era, depictions of the Virgin Mary and the infant Jesus were formal, grand and majestic. Images from the late medieval and early Renaissance periods show a tender young woman with a baby, often clothed in blue. Images of Mary in the developing world more recently show her dressed in the style of the local people. Today Mary is remembered when many other saints are neglected. Festivals and shrines in Mary's honour continue to attract millions.

LEVELS OF VENERATION
Mary, the Mother of God, is universally admired by Catholic believers. The Catholic Church accords different levels of honour. The highest level is adoration, or latria, and is reserved for God and the Trinity (God the Father, God the Son and God the Holy Ghost). Veneration of the Blessed Virgin is granted the Church's second highest honour and is known as hyperdulia, as theorized by Thomas Aquinas. Veneration of the company of all other saints is known as dulia.

JOHN THE BAPTIST

JOHN THE BAPTIST DEVOTED HIS LIFE TO WARNING PEOPLE TO "REPENT, FOR THE KINGDOM OF GOD IS AT HAND". HE DECLARED THAT THE MESSIAH WOULD SOON APPEAR AMONG THEM.

KEY FACTS
Baptized Jesus
DATES: *d.c.AD 30*
BIRTH PLACE: *Nazareth*
PATRON OF: *Pilgrims to the Holy Land, Knights Hospitallers, hoteliers, birdwatchers*
FEAST DAY: *24 June, 29 August*
EMBLEM: *Lamb, cross, a scroll*

The writings of Sts Jerome and Augustine of Hippo suggested that John the Baptist was sanctified in the womb and never committed a sin. He certainly chose a life of hardship, dressing in animal skins and living on scavenged food. He devoted his life to telling people to prepare for the coming of the Messiah and his Kingdom. He must have had a charismatic personality with great energy, for he attracted a large following.

BY THE JORDAN

His youth was spent as a hermit, surviving on a diet of locusts and wild honey, a lifestyle that closely resembled that of some of the prophets of the Old Testament. Crowds came to hear him preach, and John began to baptize them

Left Saint John the Baptist *(Titian, c.1540). John may be dressed in skins and rags, but he is here presented as a powerful man and leader. The lamb lies at his feet.*

Below Salome with the Head of Saint John the Baptist *(Bernardino Luini, c.1525–30). Salome is shown as a young woman with a sly and cunning expression.*

by dipping them in the River Jordan. When Jesus came through the crowd, a dove hovered over his head and John knew Jesus was the Messiah. He then baptized Jesus, saying he was "the Lamb of God who takest away the sins of the world". In paintings, John is often shown pointing at a lamb and holding a cross.

John the Baptist was later put in prison for denouncing an incestuous marriage between the governor of Galilee, Herod Antipas, and his niece, Herodias. His stepdaughter, Salome, pleased Herod so much with her dancing that he offered her anything she wanted. At her mother's prompting, the girl requested the head of John the Baptist.

TEACHINGS

John preached about the presence of a "messianic kingdom" and the need for all to repent their sins. His lessons were rooted in the Jewish belief that one day the Almighty would send a messiah to lead the people to righteousness. Many Jews who heard John speak therefore accepted Jesus as their long-awaited leader. A large number of disciples followed John and imitated his severe ascetic mode of life. He taught them methods of prayer and meditation.

Historians believe that John the Baptist's wanderings took him to the Dead Sea. Lessons similar to his message are recorded in the Dead Sea Scrolls – papyrus writings dating from the early Christian era. John is reputedly buried in Sebaste, Samaria. His feast day is held on his birthday. However, the date of his death is also celebrated in the West on 29 August. Medieval Christians believed that through him, Christ would enter their souls.

An important saint, some of his relics are claimed to be held in St Sylvester's Church in Rome, and in Amiens, France. Many churches in Britain and Europe have been dedicated to him.

MARY MAGDALENE

LOVED FOR HER DEVOTION TO JESUS, MARY MAGDALENE IS THE GRAND EXAMPLE OF THE REFORMED SINNER. HER LIFE SHOWS THAT ANYONE MAY BE TRANSFORMED IF THEY TRULY REPENT.

Mary Magdalene was one of the many women who accompanied Jesus and the apostles on their travels, caring for them and supporting them. She was close to Jesus and played a major role in the events surrounding his death and resurrection.

REPENTANT SINNER
While Jesus was dining at the home of a Pharisee called Simon, a woman came and knelt before him. Simon was angered by this interruption from a reputed sinner, but the woman washed Jesus' feet and begged to be forgiven. Jesus told the woman that all her sins were forgiven.

MESSENGER OF CHRIST
To modern Christians, both Orthodox and Catholic, Mary Magdalene is important because she was a devoted and committed follower of Christ who witnessed some of the most significant moments of his life.

Above Detail of Mary kissing Jesus' feet from Life of Saint Mary Magdalene *(attr. to Giotto di Bondone, Palmerino di Guido and others, 14th century).*

PREACHER AND HERMIT
Eastern legend claims that, after the Resurrection, Mary Magdalene travelled to Ephesus with the Blessed Virgin and the apostle John, where she later died and was buried. According to a Western legend, however, Mary, with her sister Martha and brother Lazarus, travelled to France. They landed in Provence and proceeded to Marseilles, where they preached the Gospel. Mary is said to have retired to a nearby cave to live as a hermit. When she died, angels carried her to the oratory of St Maximus near Aix-en-Provence.

Left Mary Magdalene Reading *(attr. to Ambrosius Benson, 1540).*

THOMAS

CHIEFLY REMEMBERED AS "DOUBTING THOMAS", THIS APOSTLE NEEDED PROOF BEFORE ACCEPTING ANY TRUTH. HE WAS THE FIRST TO ACKNOWLEDGE CHRIST'S DIVINITY AFTER THE RESURRECTION.

KEY FACTS

Apostle

DATES: *1st century AD*

BIRTH PLACE: *Probably Palestine*

PATRON OF: *Architects, carpenters, surveyors, builders, sculptors*

FEAST DAY: *3 July (West)*

EMBLEM: *Incredulity, holding T-square as a builder*

Thomas questioned things but, once he was given a satisfying answer, remained firm in his belief. He asked Jesus, "Where are you going? How can we know the way?" Jesus answered, "I am the way, the truth, and the life." Fiercely loyal, Thomas was ready to die with Jesus.

The apostle is most famously known as "Doubting Thomas" because he could not believe the Resurrection of Christ. When he met the Lord after his death, Thomas asked to touch the wounds left by a soldier's lance as he hung on the cross. Christ allowed him to do so and, now convinced of the reality, Thomas became ardent in his belief. Indeed, he was the first to publicly acknowledge the divinity of Christ by calling him "My Lord and my God".

A legend says that because Thomas did not witness the Blessed Virgin's Assumption to heaven, she appeared in person to reassure him. As a token of proof, she gave him her belt.

His life after the Pentecost is mysterious. There are claims that he travelled to India where he

Below A patient Christ offers proof of his resurrection in the painting Doubting Thomas *(Gian Francesco Barbieri, 1621).*

preached and built a cathedral for a prince. Such stories are perhaps confirmed by a community of Christians in Kerala, south India, who identify themselves as the "St Thomas Christians".

In 1522, Portuguese travellers claimed to have seen his grave in Mylapore near Madras. The *Acts of Thomas*, a document from the 3rd or 4th century, says he was killed by a lance. His relics ended up in Persia (Iran), but Ortona, in Italy, also laid claim to them.

MATTHEW

THE PRESUMED AUTHOR OF THE
FIRST GOSPEL WAS A FORMER
TAX COLLECTOR.

There are few stories about Matthew, also known as Levi. Little is known too about his life as an evangelist. He is presumed to be the author of the first gospel, written in an easy style for public reading.

Matthew was a tax collector, one of the hated class of Jews who collected money on behalf of the Roman authorities. His fellow Jews not only regarded this close contact with Gentiles as unclean, but also distrusted tax-men and believed they were corrupt. When Jesus approached Matthew, and

Above Saint Matthew *from* The Book of Kells, *an illuminated manuscript,* c.AD 800.

was even prepared to eat with him, he immediately rose from his counting table and followed him.

After Christ's Ascension to heaven, Matthew became a missionary like the other apostles but his journeys are not recorded.

An apocryphal story says that Matthew was martyred in Ethiopia defending an abbess. His reputed relics were transported to Salerno in Italy via Brittany. Others say he died in Persia.

JOHN

THE DISCIPLE WHOM JESUS LOVED AND ENTRUSTED HIS MOTHER TO
AFTER HIS DEATH IS THOUGHT TO BE THE AUTHOR OF THE FOURTH
GOSPEL, THREE EPISTLES AND THE BOOK OF REVELATION.

John and James the Great were two fiery-tempered brothers, sons of Zebedee. Both were called from mending their fishing nets to follow Jesus.

John's ardour could turn him to brave and reckless endeavours. However, Jesus' faith in John was apparent at the Crucifixion. When he was facing death, Jesus put his mother, Mary, the Blessed Virgin, into John's care rather than choose anyone else.

The belief that he was a favourite disciple is confirmed by the facts of John's life. He was with Jesus at the Miracle of the Loaves and Fishes. With Peter and James, he witnessed the Transfiguration, and he was by the side of Jesus during the Agony in the Garden of Gethsemane.

John was placed at the right hand of Christ at the Last Supper, and he was the only disciple not to desert Jesus during the horrors of the Crucifixion. He kept vigil

Left This woodcarving depicts John's anguish at the crucifixion (Ferdinand Maximilian Brokof, 18th century).

at the foot of the Cross, and then showed no hesitation in accepting Jesus had risen from the dead.

After the Ascension, John worked with St Peter organizing the early Christian Church. After some years, he was exiled to Patmos, a Greek island. One of the greatest Christian evangelists, it is thought he died at a great age in Ephesus, Turkey.

MARK

THE AUTHOR OF THE SECOND GOSPEL INTERPRETED AND RECORDED PETER'S TEACHING.

Mark was young when he first met Jesus. His mother's house was a favourite meeting place for the apostles and Jesus often visited.

Although Mark was not an apostle, he seems to have been charming and affectionate, though not brave or confident. It was rumoured that he ran away from the Roman soldiers who arrested Jesus. And he abandoned a difficult mission with St Peter to Cyprus. But when older, he gave St Paul much support during his arrest in Rome. St Peter even referred to him fondly as his son.

Mark travelled widely as an evangelist, visiting Jerusalem, Rome and Egypt. He may have travelled to Alexandria and become the first bishop of that city. Mark's gospel incorporates many of Peter's teachings and memoirs, so it is likely it was written in Rome where the two men spent long periods together.

Despite Mark's important role in the Christian story as the writer of the Second Gospel, his place and manner of death are uncertain. He is thought to have died sometime after Jerusalem was destroyed in AD 70. A legend claims he was tied round the neck and dragged through the streets of Alexandria. His bodily relics were carried by the Venetians to Venice where they were placed in the basilica named after him, St Mark's Basilica.

Right St Mark's famous emblem, the winged lion, sits at his feet (the Ulm Master, 1442).

The relics survived a fire in the church in AD 976, and were installed in the new building. A series of mosaics in the church tell the story of St Mark and the translation of his relics.

Left A statue of St Mark by the early Renaissance sculptor Donatello (1411–15). St Mark's image appears widely in Italy.

His emblem is a winged lion. This refers to the inspiration Mark derived from John the Baptist, who lived in the wilderness with animals. Mark became the patron saint of Venice. His lion emblem can be found on the façades of many buildings across the Greek Ionian islands, where medieval Venice held dominion.

LUKE

THE PHYSICIAN AND WRITER OF THE THIRD GOSPEL WAS A MOST SYMPATHETIC MAN WHO, UNUSUALLY FOR THE TIME, INCLUDED IN HIS WORK THE WOMEN WHO WERE IMPORTANT IN THE LIFE OF JESUS.

KEY FACTS
Writer of the Third Gospel
DATES: *1st century* AD
BIRTH PLACE: *Antioch, Syria*
PATRON OF: *Surgeons, doctors, painters and glass artists*
FEAST DAY: *18 October*
EMBLEM: *Winged ox*

St Luke was a Greek doctor. His writings contain observations of women and human suffering, and reveal him to be gentle and sensitive. St Paul probably converted Luke, a Gentile of Antioch, and persuaded him to travel with him on evangelical voyages around the Mediterranean.

More than any other New Testament writer, Luke shows us the women in Jesus' life. Thanks to him, we know more about Mary Magdalene and about the widow whose son Jesus restored to life. Luke tells the story of Mary and

Above This enamel plaque showing St Luke was made in the workshop of the Kremlin (17th century).

the Annunciation, and also mentions Elizabeth, mother of John the Baptist. He is deeply respectful of the Virgin Mary and apparently knew her. The words he puts into her mouth when he describes the Annunciation are known as "Mary's Prayer", and have become part of the liturgy.

A HUMANE APPROACH

Luke emphasizes gentle aspects of the faith. He repeats the most moving parables that Jesus told to show examples of goodness and kindness. However, his gospel does open with the story of the bull sacrificed by Zachary to celebrate the birth of his son, John the Baptist. This accounts for Luke's emblem, a winged ox.

He also wrote *The Acts of the Apostles*, a mixture of history and prophecy describing the spread of Christianity. He explains how the faith broke with Judaism, and extended beyond Jerusalem to Rome in the West.

Luke also has a reputation as a painter. There are many portraits of the Virgin attributed to St Luke in the Christian world, though unfortunately none are authenticated. The church of St Augustine in Rome has several such portraits. It is said Luke lived to a great age and never married.

Below St Luke Drawing the Virgin *(Rogier van der Weyden, 15th century). Luke was a talented painter as well as writer.*

STEPHEN

THE FIRST CHRISTIAN MARTYR WAS CRUELLY STONED TO DEATH IN JERUSALEM FOR HIS BELIEFS.

KEY FACTS
First martyr
DATES: *d.c.AD 35*
BIRTH PLACE: *Jerusalem*
PATRON OF: *Bricklayers, stonemasons, builders, deacons*
FEAST DAY: *26 December (West)*
EMBLEM: *Stones, the palm of martyrdom, a book*

The first ever Christian martyr was a learned Jew and one of the first deacons. After his conversion, Stephen took control of almsgiving to elderly widows in his community. When he began to preach he often criticized some aspects of Jewish Mosaic law.

After Stephen had made some particularly hostile allegations, his Jewish listeners became outraged. He accused them of resisting the true Spirit and being responsible for the death of Christ.

The mob stoned him to death with the consent of a man called Saul, a Roman Jew. Saul later converted and became Paul, the great Christian leader.

Left The stoning of St Stephen as depicted in a stained glass window (St Edmundsbury Cathedral, Suffolk, England, 19th century).

EUSTACE

THE HERO OF THIS LEGEND CHASES A STAG THAT BEARS THE CROSS OF CHRIST WITHIN ITS ANTLERS. THIS EXPERIENCE LEADS TO HIS CONVERSION AND HIS UNTIMELY DEATH.

KEY FACTS
Miracle appearance of the crucifix
DATES: *Unknown*
BIRTH PLACE: *Unknown*
PATRON OF: *Hunters and those in difficult situations*
FEAST DAY: *2 November (West; officially de-canonized)*
EMBLEM: *Stag bearing a crucifix*

Fabulous stories surround the figure of St Eustace. Named Placidas at birth, he became a high-ranking Roman soldier and was a keen huntsman.

One day he stalked a stag deep in the forest. As he lifted his bow, the stag turned. A gleaming crucifix grew between its antlers. Then the stag said, "I am Jesus, whom you honour without knowing".

Placidas, his wife and children converted to Christianity and he was baptized as Eustace. They suffered many misfortunes and Eustace's faith was tested to the limits. His wife was seduced (or raped) and his children sold into slavery. Later, their luck changed for the better when Eustace was

reunited with his family in Rome. He was honoured for a military victory, but unfortunately this good luck did not last, and when he refused to make a pagan sacrifice, he and his family were thrown to the lions in the arena. The beasts refused to attack, so the entire family was burnt inside a brazen bull – a form of execution devised by the ancient Greeks, akin to being boiled alive.

Left The Vision of Saint Eustace (Albrecht Dürer, 16th century).

JAMES THE GREAT

ABANDONING HIS FISHING NETS IN ORDER TO BECOME A "FISHER OF MEN", JAMES WAS ONE OF THE EARLIEST DISCIPLES TO FOLLOW JESUS, AND THE FIRST APOSTLE MARTYR.

KEY FACTS
Apostle
DATES: *d.AD 44*
BIRTH PLACE: *Galilee*
PATRON OF: *Spain, Guatemala, Nicaragua; and, with Philip, of Uruguay*
FEAST DAY: *25 July*
EMBLEM: *Shell, sword, pilgrim's staff, pilgrim's hat*

There were two apostles named James. One became known as James the Less and the other, James the Great – so-called because he was the elder of the two. James the Great was one of the leading apostles.

James and his brother John were fishermen who abandoned their nets to follow Jesus. Both brothers were known to be quick-tempered, hence their nickname "sons of thunder".

James also had qualities of reliability, leadership and loyalty. He witnessed the major events of Christ's life. He was one of those present at the Transfiguration, and was in the garden of Gethsemane to comfort his master during his most despairing moments.

The details of James' life after the Crucifixion are uncertain. He may have gone to Judea and Samaria to spread the Christian

Above The shell and pilgrim's staff identify St James the Great (Hans Klocker, c.17th century).

Below Apostles Philip and James are often portrayed as men of learning (School of Fra Bartolommeo, c.1400).

message. But it is known that he was beheaded by Herod Agrippa in Jerusalem.

His body, it is said, was carried to the shore where a boat suddenly materialized. His disciples placed the body in this miraculous vessel and it floated to the coast of Spain. There, Christians found the relics and buried them in a forest where the city of Santiago de Compostela now stands.

The shrine containing his relics in Compostela was of great importance during the Crusades, because soldiers believed St James could grant military prowess. Santiago de Compostela remains a major site of modern pilgrimage.

GROWTH OF HIS CULTUS

According to Spanish tradition James appeared to fight the Moors when they invaded Spain in AD 844. He rode through the sky on a white horse, holding a shield bearing a red cross and a sword. With his help, the Spanish vanquished their enemy.

In the 16th century, sailors allegedly saw St James resting on a cloud. It hovered protectively over the galleons carrying early Spanish explorers across the Atlantic to the Americas. He inspired them to convert the American people they encountered. The feast day of St James the Great is celebrated in major national festivals in South America to this day.

PETER

CHRIST DESCRIBED PETER AS THE "ROCK OF THE CHURCH". AS THE LEADER OF THE APOSTLES, HE IS THE EARTHLY FATHER OF THE FAITH, AND IS SAID TO HOLD THE KEYS TO THE KINGDOM OF HEAVEN.

Peter was warm and impetuous by nature, yet also rather cautious. To his eternal shame, he was so overwhelmed by fear during the trial of Jesus that three times he denied his friendship with him. But Peter's passion and boldness made him leader of the apostles. His name, Cephas in Aramaic, means "rock" and Jesus chose him as the "rock" upon which the Church was built.

Known as Simon Peter, he fished with his brother Andrew on the Sea of Galilee. Jesus came to them one day and said "Come with me and I will make you fishers of men." After this, Peter began his ministry with Jesus, and is mentioned frequently throughout the gospels.

Below Peter enthroned and six scenes from the lives of Jesus and St Peter (the Master of St Peter, 1280).

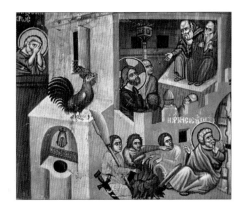

Above A mural showing Peter's denial of Christ and the cock crowing (from the Church of the Holy Cross at Platanistasa, Cyprus, 15th century).

Peter was very close to Christ and at his arrest sliced off the ear of Judas Iscariot. He was one of three apostles to witness the Transfiguration, when Jesus was surrounded by light, and was the first disciple to speak to the crowds after Pentecost.

KEY FACTS

Leader of the apostles; called the rock of the Church by Jesus
DATES: *d.c.AD 64*
BIRTH PLACE: *Bethsaida, Sea of Galilee*
PATRON OF: *Fishermen, papacy*
FEAST DAY: *29 June*
EMBLEM: *Keys, ship, fish, cockerel*

FIRST CHURCH LEADER

Peter took administrative control of the apostles after Christ's death. He sent Paul and Barnabas to the Mediterranean as disciples and evangelists, and was the first apostle to perform a miracle. More significantly, he was ready to sit at a meal with a non-Jew, or Gentile and converted a Roman centurion, Cornelius, the first Gentile to become a Christian believer.

Some authorities credit Peter with introducing the concept of "episcopal succession", choosing leaders from men who were familiar with the first apostles. This gave rise to the tradition that bishops and priests had a special closeness to Christ.

When Peter visited Rome, he was arrested for his Christian activities and tried by the Emperor Nero, who condemned him to death by crucifixion. Legend has it that Peter asked to be hung upside down on the cross because he was not worthy of dying in the same way as Christ.

Peter was buried in a tomb beneath the Vatican. He shares 29 June as a feast day with St Paul. Believers consider him the keeper of the gates to heaven, the saint who can let them enter the kingdom, or deny them entry when they die. Peter's enduring popularity is shown by the dedication of 1,129 churches to him in England alone.

ANDREW

PETER'S BROTHER ANDREW WAS THE FIRST OF THE DISCIPLES JESUS
CALLED. THE CRUEL MANNER OF HIS REPUTED MARTYRDOM ON A
SALTIRE CROSS IS COMMEMORATED ON THE SCOTTISH FLAG.

KEY FACTS
Apostle
DATES: *d.c.AD 60*
BIRTH PLACE: *Bethsaida, Galilee*
PATRON OF: *Scotland, Greece
and Russia, fishermen*
FEAST DAY: *30 November*
EMBLEM: *Small saltire cross*

Andrew heard John the Baptist preach and longed to meet Jesus. He and his brother Peter (then called Simon), worked as fishermen on the Sea of Galilee.

Initially, the brothers only joined Jesus at his preaching from time to time. But finally they abandoned their families and their work to follow him. The Greek Orthodox Church calls Andrew "Protoclete", meaning "first-called". They venerate him highly, as do the Roman Catholic and Russian Orthodox Churches.

Jesus granted the Miraculous Draught of Fishes to Andrew and Peter. This occurred when, after a day of poor fishing, the presence of Jesus produced a great haul for the two men. Andrew also played a part in the feeding of the 5,000 with loaves and fishes. Being an intense believer, he encouraged Gentiles to meet the Messiah, too.

MISSION AND DEATH

After the Crucifixion, it seems much of Andrew's mission work was in Greece, but he also went to Constantinople (Istanbul), a key place in the history of the early Church. Medieval worshippers claim he founded the Church there. Some believe he preached as far as Kiev in Ukraine before moving on to Scotland, but there is no evidence for this.

Legend gives Andrew a brave martyrdom at Patras. With dignity, he disrobed himself and knelt before the cross as his persecutors prepared him for crucifixion. He was bound to the wooden beams

Above Martyrdom of the Apostle Andreas *from Westphalia (artist unknown, c.1500).*

of the saltire (X-shaped) cross. Even in his agony, Andrew is said to have carried on preaching. The crowd begged the consul to show mercy and take the dying man down. This he did after two days.

In 1204, Crusaders siezed Constantinople and took St Andrew's supposed relics to Amalfi, Italy. However, some say that St Regulus journeyed "to the ends of the earth" carrying his relics. Then an angel led him to Scotland, to the place now named after him, St Andrews.

Below St Andrew and St Peter Responding to the Call of Jesus, *Byzantine mosaic (6th century).*

PAUL

INITIALLY A PERSECUTOR OF CHRISTIANS, AFTER HIS DRAMATIC CONVERSION PAUL BECAME THE CHURCH'S FIRST MISSIONARY. HIS LETTERS DEVELOPED AND EXPOUNDED CHRISTIAN THEOLOGY.

On meeting Paul, a Roman centurion was struck by the apostle's air of nobility and courage. Others described him as having the spirit of a strong man who was generous and eager to create a cheerful atmosphere.

Paul was Jewish-born, in Tarsus, and was named Saul. His upbringing was steeped in strict Jewish Law but his family had also been granted Roman citizenship.

CONVERSION

As a zealous Jew and Roman, Saul was active in the repression of the new Jewish heresy that followed the crucified Jesus. On one such errand Saul was travelling along the road to Damascus when suddenly he was blinded by a great light and overcome by the presence of Jesus. He understood from this vision that his mission was to spread the Christian faith to Gentile, non-Jewish people.

After being baptized he spent several years in Arabia living as a hermit then returned to Damascus and began to preach about Jesus, taking the name of Paul as a mark of his change. His preaching, however, aroused the fury of local Jews. Paul was forced to escape with the help of fellow disciples who lowered him in a basket over the city wall.

He travelled to Jerusalem to meet Peter who chose him and Barnabas as travelling evangelists.

APOSTLE TO THE GENTILES

At the Council of Jerusalem in about AD 50 Paul argued that the Church should be as catholic

Above This portrait of St Paul captures the expression of a noble man (Etienne Parrocel, c.1740s).

Below Paul travelling on the road to Damascus with his troops in search of Christians to persecute in The Conversion of St Paul *(Pieter Bruegel the elder, 1567).*

KEY FACTS
Great missionary and theologian
DATES: *d.AD 64–65*
BIRTH PLACE: *Tarsus in Cilicia*
PATRON OF: *Malta, Greece, Catholic missions and lay teachers*
FEAST DAY: *29 June*
EMBLEM: *Sword and book; generally portrayed as elderly and balding with a long beard*

(universal) as the Roman Empire. Winning this argument possibly saved Christianity from remaining a mere sect of Judaism, and opened the way for a new belief system. Paul's teaching was intimate and personal, related to his experience of the vision of Jesus.

ARREST AND DEATH

Paul was eventually found guilty of "anti-imperial activities" and beheaded in Rome. Tradition claims he died on 29 June in AD 64 or 65, the same day as Peter, and thus they share their feast day. Paul is the first great missionary and theologian of Christianity. He is regarded as second only to Jesus in inspiring Christian faith.

CECILIA

ANGELS AND HEAVENLY MUSIC HELPED CECILIA TO CONVERT HER HUSBAND AND OTHERS.

KEY FACTS
Virgin martyr
DATES: *3rd century AD*
BIRTH PLACE: *Rome*
PATRON OF: *Musicians, singers, composers*
FEAST DAY: *22 November*
EMBLEM: *Organ or lute*

When she was a young woman, Cecilia's family refused to accept that she had taken a vow of virginity and forced her to marry a pagan. During the wedding, Cecilia sang silently to the Lord, "My heart remain unsullied, so that I may not be confounded". The bride vowed that her marriage would never be consummated.

Cecilia kept strong in her faith and told her husband, Valerian, that an angel was guarding her. She said God would be angry if Valerian touched her, but if he desisted, God would love him. Furthermore, if her husband were baptized, he would see this angel.

Valerian converted and angels appeared and placed flowers on the heads of the young couple. Cecilia's brother Tiburtius chose to become a Christian after this incident. In fact, the two men became so ardent in their faith that the Romans beheaded them, as Christianity was proscribed. Cecilia buried the two martyrs at her home. She, too, attracted anger

Above A terracotta statue of Cecilia in the cathedral in Le Mans, France (Charles Hoyay, 17th century).

from the state, but officials sent to arrest her were so overwhelmed by her faith that they converted.

Cecilia converted 400 people who were later baptized by Pope Urban in her home, which was later dedicated as a church.

The authorities did not abandon their persecution of Cecilia. They tried locking her in her own bathroom and burning the furnaces high. She lived through this ordeal, and then survived for three days after a soldier hacked at her neck with a sword.

There is little firm evidence for Cecilia's story. Her patronage of music comes from the heavenly sound she heard in her head while the organs played at her wedding.

ANASTASIA

Virgin martyrs such as Ursula and Cecilia have attracted legends of heroism and miracles. Other martyrs give their names to churches, or else linger in the religious folk memory.

One such figure is St Anastasia. Nothing is known about her. It is possible she was martyred at a place now known as Srem Mitrovica, Serbia. Her name is in the Roman Canon. A prayer is said to her at Mass, and a few antique Byzantine churches carry her name. She was a "matron", not a "maiden", so she is not counted as one of the virgin martyrs.

Below A stained-glass window depicting the martyrdom of St Anastasia (20th-century copy from a 13th-century original).

Left St Cecilia's tomb. Her body was found lying in this position in 1599, and the statue copies it exactly.

GEORGE

THE POTENCY OF HIS STORY ENSURES THAT ST GEORGE HOLDS A PLACE IN THE COMPANY OF SAINTS, BUT THE CHURCH SUSPECTS THAT THIS CHIVALROUS KNIGHT MAY BE MERELY A LEGEND.

KEY FACTS
Knight martyr
DATES: *d.c.AD 303*
BIRTH PLACE: *Cappadocia, Turkey*
PATRON OF: *England, Istanbul, boy scouts, soldiers, and many other groups*
FEAST DAY: *23 April*
EMBLEM: *Red cross on white background, dragon*

In the 6th century, St George was described as good in so many ways that all his "deeds are known only to God". Sadly, most things about this saint remain known only by his maker, because evidence of his life is so sparse.

It seems certain, however, that George was a real martyr, a knight who came from Cappadocia in Turkey and died in Lydda (site of modern-day Lod) in Palestine.

Above St George as depicted in a fresco in the Church of our Lady of the Pasture, Asinou, Cyprus (late 12th century).

GEORGE AND THE DRAGON

In what is undoubtedly his most famous legend, George was riding through Libya when he heard cries of mourning. Townspeople told him that they were being tyrannized by a dragon that they had to feed with two lambs a day. Now they had no lambs left and the dragon was demanding a human meal. They had drawn lots from the maidens and the king's daughter had been chosen. Dressed in a beautiful bridal gown, the princess had gone forth to meet her doom. St George dashed into action and crippled the monster by thrusting his lance into it. Tying her girdle round the dragon's neck, the princess led it limping to the town. The terrified citizens prepared to run, but George told them that if they would be baptized, the dragon would be slain. They all agreed. It was alleged that approximately 15,000 people were baptized. Four ox carts moved the beast's body to a distant meadow.

Right St George and the Dragon (Paolo Uccello, c.1439–40).

CULTUSES AND CRUSADES

There are signs that St George's cultus was widespread early in Christian history. He was venerated across Europe and known in England before the Norman Conquest of AD 1066. His image can be found all over the Middle East, the Balkans and Greece.

During the Crusader battle of Antioch in AD 1098, Frankish (German) knights were blessed with a vision of George and another knight, St Demetrius. Possibly on his return from the Third Crusade a century later, Richard I promoted the veneration of St George in England.

PATRONAGE

St George is now the patron saint of England, as well as of boy scouts and soldiers, and many churches bear his name. In 1914, together with St John Chrysostom and St Roch, St George was declared a patron of Constantinople (Istanbul).

Because so little is actually known of St George, the Church downgraded him in 1960, and today his feast day is reduced to prayers during mass. But his name and his story of chivalry are loved across the world. His flag, a red cross on white background, was well known by the 14th century and is the national flag of England.

CHRISTOPHER

THE PATRON SAINT OF TRAVELLERS DERIVES HIS NAME FROM A GREEK WORD MEANING "ONE WHO CARRIES CHRIST". CHRISTOPHER IS LOVED FOR THIS HONOURABLE TASK.

KEY FACTS
Carried the child Jesus across a river
DATES: *Unknown*
BIRTH PLACE: *Unknown*
PATRON OF: *Wayfarers, travellers and motorists*
FEAST DAY: *25 July*
EMBLEM: *Pole to aid walking through the river, carrying a child on his shoulder*

One of the best-known saints, Christopher is now deemed legendary and no longer included in the Roman Calendar. However, this "de-canonization" has not stopped the popular veneration of St Christopher, whose image adorns cars and key rings. Travellers everywhere continue to pray for his intercession.

According to some stories, Christopher was a tall, muscular man. He is described in the *Golden Legend* as having a "fearful face and appearance".

Below This image from a German illuminated manuscript gives a realistic view of the agony St Christopher endured as he carried the small, but extraordinarily heavy infant Jesus across the river (15th century).

BECOMING A CHRISTIAN

Christopher found "a right great king" to serve, but soon observed he made the sign of the cross whenever hearing the word "devil". Christopher felt that needing such help was hardly fitting for a great monarch. So instead, he sought this powerful devil and worked for him.

With the devil leading him, Christopher travelled through the desert. The discovery that a cross, thrust into the sands, frightened the devil prompted Christopher to seek an explanation. A holy hermit told him about the power of this cross, and then converted him to Christianity.

Because of his size, Christopher dreaded fasting. Nor could he accept long hours of prayer and short periods of sleep. The hermit asked if Christopher could carry travellers across the river. In this way, the *Golden Legend* explains, he found a way to serve the Lord.

CARRYING CHRIST

A child once asked Christopher to carry him, so he hoisted the little boy on to his shoulders and stepped into the water. The child grew heavier, but Christopher persevered. On reaching the other bank, he felt "all the world upon me; I might bear no greater burden". The boy replied, "Thou hast not only borne all the world upon thee, but thou hast borne Him that made all the world, upon thy soldiers. I am Jesus Christ."

Christopher went to Lycia (southern Turkey) to preach but was arrested. He survived burning by iron rods, and when they shot him, the arrows stopped in mid-air. Finally they beheaded him.

The truth about Christopher is sparse. He was martyred in the Middle East, honoured in the 3rd century AD, and a church was dedicated to him in the 4th century AD. Early Christians prayed to his image to ensure safe travel, which has led to the practice today.

Below St Christopher is gaunt but noble in this sensitive wood carving (Gothic-style winged altar in the Kefermarkt, Austria, c.1490).

JEROME

THE GREATEST BIBLICAL SCHOLAR OF HIS TIME WAS VENERATED FOR HIS AUTHORITATIVE TRANSLATION OF THE BIBLE FROM THE ORIGINAL HEBREW AND GREEK VERSIONS INTO LATIN.

Numerous paintings of Jerome show a lean old man, bent over his books in a remote cave. At his feet a lion keeps benevolent guard. But the reality was quite different. Jerome seems to have been a man at war with himself. He longed to concentrate on his studies but also sought academic debate. A quick temper made this saint unpleasantly aggressive and intolerant of his colleagues' ideas.

EARLY LIFE
Jerome received a classical education, went on to study further in Rome, and then travelled widely searching for teachers and further intellectual stimulation.

At this early stage in his life Jerome was not devout, being more interested in the literature and philosophy of the Greeks. However when travelling with two friends, all three men fell dangerously ill. The death of both his

KEY FACTS
One of the four great Latin Doctors of the Western Church
DATES: *c.AD 341–420*
BIRTH PLACE: *Strido, Dalmatia (Balkans)*
PATRON OF: *Scholars, students, archaeologists, librarians, translators*
FEAST DAY: *30 September*
EMBLEM: *Bishop's hat, book, stone and lion*

Left St Jerome *(Theodoricus of Prague, 14th century). Often his symbol in art is a book.*

companions had a profound impact on Jerome, who turned to the Christian faith. But his commitment to Christianity caused him great anguish. He greatly enjoyed the company of women, and found too much pleasure in reading pagan Greek texts. Believing these joys would carry him away from God, he decided to abstain from them. To this end, Jerome went to live as a hermit in the desert where he could think and pray without distraction.

GREAT SCHOLAR
Somewhat against his will, he was ordained and sent back to Rome in AD 382. Posterity honours him for translating the Bible from Greek and Hebrew into Latin. His version is known as the Vulgate or Authorized Bible.

SCANDAL AND FLIGHT
Forced to flee Rome after being accused of intimacy with female students, Jerome travelled to Cyprus and Antioch where the widow Paula and her daughter, joined him. Together they went to Egypt, then to Bethlehem. Paula established three nunneries in Bethlehem, and she built a monastery for men which Jerome headed for a while before retiring to a cave nearby, where he continued to create controversy among fellow theologians. It is said he died with his head resting on the manger where Jesus was born.

Left Saint Jerome in a Landscape *(Giovanni Battista Cima da Conegliano, c.1500–1510).*

BENEDICT

ST BENEDICT CREATED A MONASTIC LIFE OF SIMPLICITY, WORK AND PRAYER FOR THE RELIGIOUS. HIS RULES REJECTED THE GRIM HARDSHIP IMPOSED BY FOUNDERS OF MORE AUSTERE ORDERS.

KEY FACTS
Founder
DATES: c.*AD 480–550*
BIRTH PLACE: *Norcia, Italy*
PATRON OF: *Europe*
FEAST DAY: *11 July*
EMBLEM: *Black gown of his order, Rule book, broken cup containing poison*

The best way to appreciate the character of St Benedict is by studying his Rule. These guides to daily living reveal a man who understood the perils of power. He knew that extreme forms of discipline were unkind and could even drive men and women mad.

Born in Umbria, Italy, some time in the 5th century AD, Benedict was sent as a student to Rome. However, he disliked the riotous living of the city and lived in a cave by the ruins of Nero's palace spending most of his time in prayer and meditation. Gradually, his fame spread.

Left Saint Benedict with His Monks at the Refectory *(Il Sodoma, c.1505).*

MONASTIC BEGINNINGS
Benedict was persuaded to join a nearby monastery, where he was disturbed by the lax, even dissolute, ways of the monks, and set about reforming them. This caused hostility and Benedict returned to the life of a hermit, where disciples gathered about him. Benedict founded 12 small monasteries. The houses gained a reputation for simple, learned living, without enforced austerity.

RULE OF THE ORDER
Benedict perceived that prayer, routine and purposeful activity were the paths to God. Authority was to be controlled and shared. A simple, vegetarian but ample diet was served. Benedict allowed sensible hours of sleep. Property was communal, and the monks had to work, either producing food, maintaining the monastery, or writing the scriptures. But more important than any other duty was regular communal prayer.

It was this kindly, humane interpretation of the monastic life that made Benedict so popular, and which still operates today.

Left St Benedict, *shown wearing the black garb of his monastic order (Pietro Perugino, c.1495–98).*

FRANCIS OF ASSISI

THROUGHOUT THE WORLD TODAY, FRANCISCAN MONKS AND NUNS CONTINUE THE CHARITY WORK BEGUN BY THEIR FOUNDER, WHOSE PURE LOVE OF CREATION INSPIRED A NEW ATTITUDE TO THE WORLD.

KEY FACTS

First saint to receive the stigmata, in 1224
DATES: *1181–1226*
BIRTH PLACE: *Assisi, Italy*
PATRON OF: *Animals and birds, ecologists, merchants*
FEAST DAY: *4 October*

Few saints are held in such high esteem for their spirit of devotion as is St Francis. The humble friar wished for nothing other than to imitate Christ. For him the world was an expression of God, and this conviction gave him a special affinity with nature.

REJECTING WEALTH

Francis was born into a rich Italian family and as a youth enjoyed his privileged status. But later started to give away money to the poor and once, so overcome with compassion, he kissed the diseased hand of a leper.

His father was so angry at this bizarre behaviour that he demanded his son renounce his inheritance. Francis was glad to do

Left Scenes from the life of St Francis of Assisi *(Bonaventura Berlinghieri, 1235). This is the earliest known depiction of Francis.*

so, for he had heard a voice telling him to live without property, and he left his family to take up a life of poverty.

NEW ORDER

Francis lived in a bare hut, and cared for the local lepers. His preaching and devotion attracted followers, impressed by the simplicity and humility of Francis's faith. In 1210, Pope Innocent III authorized Francis and 11 companions to be "roving preachers of God". The order soon spread across Europe as far as England.

Despite poor health, Francis made several journeys to convert Muslims living around the Mediterranean Sea. In 1219, he reached the Holy Land, but the following year the Franciscans recalled him to Europe.

SPIRITUAL RETREAT

Elias of Cortona now maintained the Franciscan Rule, which insisted on possessing no money or property, teaching the word of Christ, and caring for the sick. In 1224, Francis retreated to the Apennine Mountains where he fasted for 40 days with his followers. While there he received the stigmata on his hands, feet and side. In 1226, blind yet filled with joyous faith, Francis died at Portiuncula.

Above St Francis Prays to the Birds, *fresco from the church of San Francesco in Assisi (c.1260).*

JOAN OF ARC

AS THE GIRL WARRIOR, JOAN OF ARC, PERISHED IN THE FIRE PREPARED BY ENGLISHMEN, ONE SOLDIER WAS HEARD TO CRY OUT, "WE ARE LOST. WE HAVE BURNED A SAINT."

KEY FACTS
Visionary, military leader
DATES: *c. 1412–31*
BIRTH PLACE: *Domrémy, France*
PATRON OF: *France, French soldiers*
FEAST DAY: *30 May*
EMBLEM: *Armour, battle banner*

Joan of Arc was courageous and indifferent to pain, a fine horse-woman and deft with her sword, but began life as an illiterate peasant. How did she convince a royal court that she could be a military leader? Where did she learn to lead an army?

Brought up in the Champagne area of France during the Hundred Years War between England and France, Joan grew up in a war-torn environment. Her village was sympathetic to the royal house of Orléans. But across the river, the peasants sided with the dukes of Burgundy and the English. When she was 13, Joan said she heard God speak to her. As a result, she vowed to remain a virgin, devoted to Christ.

DIVINE VOICES

At 16, Joan claimed frequent visits by the archangel Michael and two saints, Catherine of Alexandria and Margaret of Antioch who told her to crown the dauphin,

Below Joan of Arc Kissing the Sword of Deliverance *(Dante Gabriel Rossetti, 1863).*

Charles, as King of France. At court the young royal listened to her announcement that God had sent her to help him and his kingdom. After close questioning from religious and military leaders, Joan won permission to raise arms and prepared for battle bearing a banner painted with the words "Jesus Maria". The people of nearby Vaucouleurs gave her a horse and a suit of white armour.

On 7 May 1429, Joan led her soldiers into war and banished the English from Orléans. She went on to win victories in Patay and Tours as well, and stood beside the dauphin as he was crowned King Charles VII of France in July. Joan continued the fight, but was captured by the Burgundians who sold her to the English.

WITCHCRAFT

Joan was charged with witchcraft and heresy, found guilty and sentenced to be burned. Her corpse was displayed to the crowd to prove she was a woman who had "wickedly" paraded as a man.

To prevent any veneration of the relics, her ashes were thrown into the River Seine. but in 1456, the pope overturned the guilty verdict. For centuries she was popularly held to be a saint but the Church waited until 1920 before granting canonization.

Joan is the first Christian patriot, her love of country entwined with her religion.

IGNATIUS OF LOYOLA

AS FOUNDER OF THE POWERFUL MISSIONARY ORDER, THE SOCIETY OF JESUS (ALSO KNOWN AS THE JESUITS), ST IGNATIUS SPEARHEADED THE COUNTER-REFORMATION IN EUROPE.

KEY FACTS
Founder of the Society of Jesus,
or "Jesuits"
DATES: *c.1491–1556*
BIRTH PLACE: *Azpeitia, Spain*
PATRON OF: *Spiritual exercise*
and retreats
FEAST DAY: *31 July*
EMBLEM: *Black cassock, heart*
pierced by thorns, the monogram
of Christ (HIS), and a crown
of glory

The youngest of 11 children of a noble Basque family, Ignatius was born in the Castle of Loyola at Azpeitia. He followed the course taken by many young men of the period and trained as a soldier in the Spanish army.

Convalescing after a severe wound to his leg while fighting the French at Pamplona, Ignatius is said to have had a vision of Mary, the Blessed Virgin, with Jesus beside her. The experience inspired him to go to the Benedictine abbey at Montserrat, where he laid his sword and dagger upon the altar, and took up life as a hermit in a nearby cave.

TRAINING THE SPIRIT

Ignatius imposed a harsh lifestyle on himself, going without food for long periods and scourging his body daily. As word spread, people started visiting him to seek his advice and join him in prayer.

At the age of 32, Ignatius walked to Jerusalem, where he hoped to convert Muslims but the Franciscan brothers discouraged him and sent him home. Back in Barcelona, he took up studying and began to preach. However, since he was no priest, this did not endear him to the Church.

SOLDIERS OF CHRIST

In Paris to do further studies, the ambitious young man formed a brotherhood with six friends.

Having now been ordained, Ignatius instructed the group using his own spiritual manual, *Spiritual Exercises*. This work consisted of a four-week course

designed to induct new "soldiers of Christ", as Ignatius refered to the members of his brotherhood. They gave themselves to chastity and poverty, and determined to teach those without education.

Calling themselves the Society of Jesus, or Jesuits, they pledged to conduct missions in Europe to reclaim souls lost to the Protestant reformers. The pope gave the society his blessing in 1540, and Ignatius was chosen as its general.

RETRIEVING CATHOLICS

Ignatius spent the rest of his life in Rome. He founded a house for converted Jews, and hostels for prostitutes. But it was his work in organizing foreign missions that earned his reputation. His writing and teaching played a pivotal role in drawing believers back to the Roman Catholic Church after the Reformation.

His conviction in the power of prayer and sympathy towards those struggling with Christian principles endeared him to

Right Detail of The Vision of St Ignatius of Loyola *(Peter Paul Rubens, 17th century).*

Left St Francis Borgia Helping a Dying Impenitent *(Francisco José de Goya y Lucientes, 1795).*

believers. His influence over Church doctrine and teaching has been immense.

Yet Ignatius was criticized in some quarters for being too militaristic and authoritarian. Likewise, the Jesuits, as they were popularly known, have been attacked for their power and political meddling.

Under Ignatius' leadership, the society grew rapidly. By his death, after 16 years of development, the number of Jesuits had increased to more than 1,000 members.

THERESA OF ÁVILA

THIS DEVOUT NUN COURTED CONTROVERSY DURING HER LIFETIME BY CHALLENGING THE ESTABLISHED CARMELITE ORDER AND BY CLAIMING NUMEROUS VISIONS AND COMMUNICATIONS WITH CHRIST.

KEY FACTS
Mystic, virgin
DATES: *1515–82*
BIRTH PLACE: *Avila, Spain*
PATRON OF: *Spain, Spanish Catholic writers, Carmelites*
FEAST DAY: *15 October*
EMBLEM: *Pen and book, an angel, burning lance or arrow*

Theresa de Capeda y Ahumada was born at Ávila to a wealthy Castilian family. She was a bright, independent girl whose piety was evident from an early age. After her mother's death, her father sent her to an Augustinian convent, where she discovered her calling to the Church. Aged 20, and against her father's wishes, she entered a Carmelite convent. Following the death of her father in 1543, Theresa became committed to a private, contemplative life.

VISIONARY

After collapsing in front of an image of Christ she realized she must renounce all worldly emotion and live only for Him. From that time Theresa had visions and went into deep spiritual trances

Below Theresa of Ávila's Vision of a Dove *(Peter Paul Rubens, c.1614).*

Above Detail of the Ecstasy of Saint Theresa, *held in the Church of Santa Maria della Vittoria in Rome (Gianlorenzo Bernini, c.1645–52).*

when she prayed. She felt misunderstood by her fellow nuns who were dismissive of her mystic experiences. For the rest of her life she continued to have rapturous visions. In particular, she suffered a pain in her side, inflicted, she claimed, by an angel who thrust a burning lance into her heart. Her powers of contemplation developed into a deep devotion and she referred to herself as "Theresa of Jesus".

REFORMER

After meeting Peter of Alcantara, Theresa was moved to follow his example of strict penance and mental prayer. She requested permission from the pope to open a small house. The order would be named St Joseph after her patron saint. When the secret plans were revealed, the Carmelite nuns and influential people of Ávila asked the pope to stop them. Theresa appealed to Spain's King Philip II, who resented Rome's authority. This caused angry confrontation between Church and state and Theresa was imprisoned for two years before she was permitted to open a Carmelite sub-group known as Discalced, or Barefoots. They were separated from the world, lived on alms, forbidden to eat meat, and were instructed by Theresa in meditation.

During the next few years, Theresa travelled across Spain establishing convents. She founded 16 convents and 14 monasteries, because men, too, wanted to take the vows of the Discalced. These male orders were organized with the help of another mystic, John of the Cross.

Theresa's writings are testament to her great personal devotion and her thoughts on a life of prayer. Chief among her works are *The Interior Castle* and *The Way of Perfection*, which continue to be published in numerous languages.

Theresa of Ávila died at the convent of Alba de Tormes. The odour of violets and sweet oil emanated from her tomb. Theresa was canonized by Pope Gregory XV in 1622, and declared a Doctor of the Church in 1970, the first woman to win this recognition. Her order continues to prove the need for retreat and prayer in the modern world.

BERNADETTE OF LOURDES

BERNADETTE HAD VISIONS OF MARY, THE BLESSED VIRGIN, BUT IT WAS HER TRUST IN GOD THAT QUALIFIED HER AS A SAINT.

KEY FACTS
Visionary
DATES: *1844–79*
BIRTH PLACE: *Lourdes, France*
FEAST DAY: *16 April (in parts of France 18 February)*

In the tradition of other saints of devout simplicity, such as Jean-Baptiste Vianney and Joseph of Copertino, Bernadette Soubirous was deeply spiritual and blessed by heavenly visions. And, as with those great men, she bore her role with dignity.

Bernadette was a country girl, the eldest of six children born to an impoverished miller in the Basque region of France. As a child, she was thin and stunted from lack of proper nutrition and suffered from asthma.

VISIONS OF MARY

When she was 14 years old, Bernadette experienced her first vision at the rock of Massabielle near Lourdes. Over the next six months, the same apparition of a beautiful young woman appeared

Above Since Bernadette's visions at Lourdes, many ill pilgrims visit the site in the hope that they will be cured.

Below The incorrupt body of Bernadette of Lourdes, kept at the convent in Nevers, where she lived for many years.

to her 18 times. No one else saw or heard the vision, but there were witnesses to Bernadette's reactions as they occurred. The vision informed Bernadette that the beautiful woman was Mary of the Immaculate Conception and instructed her to drink from the nearby spring and show penitence.

Church clerics and minor state officials interrogated Bernadette for months. Her answers, simple and unchanging, led some of them to label her stupid, but most were impressed by her sincerity. The resulting publicity frightened Bernadette, but she faced the jokes and cruel jibes, showing no anger. No matter how remorseless the goading became, she never denied her miraculous experience.

In 1866, she joined the Sisters of Notre-Dame of Nevers, and found merciful seclusion from the public. Her health was poor and she spent her remaining years in stoic suffering. Bernadette was canonized in 1933, in recognition of her patience, integrity, simplicity and devout trustfulness.

A PILGRIMAGE CENTRE

Secluded in the convent, Bernadette was unaware that the site where she had met the Blessed Virgin was being transformed into a pilgrimage centre, or that the basilica built there was consecrated in 1876, three years before her death.

Lourdes has become one of the great pilgrimage centres of the Christian faith, drawing to its miraculous waters those seeking spiritual healing.

THERESA OF LISIEUX

THERESA, THE "LITTLE FLOWER", WROTE OF HER RELATIONSHIP WITH GOD WITH AN ARTLESS SIMPLICITY THAT CONVEYED A DEEP SPIRITUALITY, QUALIFYING HER AS A DOCTOR OF THE CHURCH.

KEY FACTS
Virgin, mystic, Doctor of the Church
DATES: *1873–1897*
BIRTH PLACE: *Alençon, France*
PATRON OF: *France, missions, florists and flower growers*
FEAST DAY: *1 October*
EMBLEM: *Flowers*

Theresa of Lisieux lived a very ordinary life. She did not perform great works, found a religious order or convert thousands to Christianity, and yet she left a rich spiritual legacy.

AN EARLY VOCATION
Although she was only four years old when her mother died, Theresa had four older sisters to look after her. The eldest, Pauline, became her surrogate mother, but by the time Theresa was ten, her two eldest sisters had left home to enter the local Carmelite convent in Lisieux.

At the age of 15, in April 1888, Theresa joined her sisters and began a life in the enclosed Carmelite convent, where she began to develop her spirituality by reading the Carmelite mystics

Above Theresa of Lisieux (artist and date unknown). Aware she was dying, Theresa wrote that, after her death, she would "let fall a shower of roses", meaning that in heaven she would intercede for her friends.

and following the austere rules of the order. The abbess forbade Theresa to fast because she was not physically robust, but she sensed that the young girl was an intuitive thinker, and encouraged her to write. This wise advice allowed Theresa the time and space to produce *The Story of a Soul*, and her many other texts, which include 54 poems, 20 prayers, eight plays and more than 200 letters. In a simple poetic style, these writings describe how every "little life" can be enhanced by faith and reveal her extraordinary relationship with God.

Left A photograph of Theresa of Lisieux in the garden of the Carmelite convent in Lisieux in France (c.1890).

THE "LITTLE WAY"
Theresa longed to be a saint, and searched for a path that would lead to sanctity. "I knew I was a very little soul who could offer only little things to the good God", she wrote. From this grew her "little way" of "the doing of the least actions for love".

Theresa wanted to follow the example of the apostles and longed for the opportunity to spread the love of Christ in foreign lands. She always prayed for Carmelite missionaries abroad, but she also wished to visit Carmelite nuns in Hanoi, Indo-China (now Vietnam).

QUIET SUFFERING
Then, in 1895 she developed tuberculosis. With her health broken, her dream of becoming a missionary would never be realized. For 18 months, Theresa suffered pain and difficulty in breathing. She was eventually confined to the convent infirmary, where she was so ill that she was unable to receive Holy Communion. She died at the age of 24.

Pilgrims still flock to Lisieux to venerate St Theresa, who is known as the "little flower of Jesus" and Theresa-of-the-Child-Jesus, names that reflect her simple, childlike faith. Her book has been translated into 50 languages and has brought inspiration to millions of people. Theresa of Lisieux was canonized in 1925.

INDEX

Page numbers in bold refer to saint's
main entry.

Acacius 51
Agnes 11, **43**
Agnes Cao Guiying 61
Alexander III, Pope 16
Alexander Nevski 56
All Saints and All Souls 35
Ambrose 12–13, 18
Anastasia **84**
Andrew 40, **82**
Antony of Egypt 13, 46
Apostles 7, 10, 37, **40–1**
art, saints in 54–5
Assumption 66
Augustine of Canterbury 46
Augustine of Hippo 13, 20, 73
Augustinians 46, 47

Barbara 17, 51
Basil the Great 15
beatification 17, 32–3
Bell, Gertrude 30
Benedict 46, **88**
Benedict XIV, Pope 13
Benedictines 46, 47
Berard, John 32
Bernadette of Lourdes 30, 63, **93**
Bernadino of Feltre 33
Black Death 50, 51
Black Madonna 19
Blaise 51
Blessed Virgin 7, 11, 14, 27, 54, **72**
    appearances 30, 49
    cult 66–7
    titles 67
Brigid of Ireland 17
Buddhism 7

Callistus, Pope 58
Calvin, John 55
Camillus of Lellis 53
canonization 6, 16–17, 29
Canute of Denmark 57
Capuchins 47
Carmelites 47, 92, 94
Cassian 46
catacombs of Rome 11
cathedrals 64

Catherine Labouré 63
Catherine of Alexandria 10, 51
Cecilia 62, **84**
Celestine V, Pope 59
Charlemagne, Holy Roman Emperor 21
Charles Lwanga 28
Chaucer, Geoffrey 31
child saints 42–3
Christopher 14, 17, 50, 51, **86**
Church 6, 7, 9, 55, 67
church architecture 64–5
Church of England 27
    Doctors of the Church 12–13
    early Church 10–11
Cistercians 47
Clare 47
Clement 19
Clement I, Pope 58
Congregation for the Causes of Saints
    17
Constantine I, Emperor 12, 22, 41
Cornelius, Pope 58
Counter-Reformation 59
Crusades 53
cultuses 16, 17, 51
Cunegund 56
Cyricus 51

Day of the Dead 35
Demetrius 52, 53
Denys of Paris 51
Desert Fathers 13, 15, 46, 47
Diocletian, Emperor 52
Discalced Carmelites 47
Doctors of the Church 12–13, 15
Dominic 47
Dominic Savio 43
Dominicans 47
Doyle, Sir Arthur Conan 11

Edmund of Abingdon 57
Edward the Confessor 56, 62
Edward the Martyr 57
Elizabeth I 27
Elizabeth II 27
Elizabeth of Hungary 57
Elizabeth of Portugal 57
Elizabeth Seton 28
Ephrem 34
Erasmus 51
Eric of Sweden 57
Ethelbert of Kent 56
Eustace 51, **79**

Fang Ho, Rev. 60
Father Joseph Damien 32
Fátima, Portugal 30
feast days 9, 24–5, 34–5
Fourteen Holy Helpers 37, 50–1
Foy (St Faith) 21, 31, 42
Fra Angelico 55
Francis of Assisi 7, 23, 28, 31, 47, **89**
Francis Regis Clet 60
Francis Xavier 28, 60
Franciscans 47
Francisco Fernandez de Capillas 60

George 7, 14, 17, 51, 52, 53, **85**
Giles 51
Gothic architecture 64
Gregory II, Pope 59
Gregory of Nazianzus 15
Gregory of Sinai 15
Gregory Palamas 15
Gregory the Great, Pope 13, 54, 55, 59
Gregory VII, Pope 59

Hadrian, Emperor 22
healing 19
Helen 22
Henry II, Holy Roman Emperor 56
Henry IV, Holy Roman Emperor 59
Henry VIII 27
hermits 13, 16, 47
heroic virtue 6
Hildegard of Bingen 18, 55
Hinduism 7
Holy Family 10, 37, **38–9**
Holy House of Loreto 20
Hyacinth Castaneda 61

icons 15
Ignatius of Loyola 47, **91**
Immaculate Conception 66
incorruptibles 62–3
Innocent III, Pope 16
Innocent III, Pope 62
Irene 11, 42
Isidore 18–19
Isidore of Seville 35

James the Great 23, 31, 40, 52, 54, 76, **80**
Januarius 10, 19, 62
Jean-Baptiste Vianney 63, 92
Jerome 12, 13, 54, 73, **87**
Jesuits 47, 91
Jesus 10, 21, 22, **38–9**, 54, 66, 67, 83

Apostles **40–1**, 75, 76, 77, 80, 81, 82
Joachim Royo 28
Joan of Arc 11, 18, 52, **90**
John 14, **76**, 80
John Chrysostom 15, 34, 85
John of God 53
John of Montecorvino 60
John Paul II, Pope 6, 13, 17, 29, 53, 61
John the Baptist 13, 19, **73**, 82
Josephine Bakhita 28–9
Juan Diego 23, 31
Judaism 7
Judas Iscariot 40, 41
Julius 53

Kateri Tekakwitha 28, 33
Kenelm 42
Knights Hospitaller of St John 46, 47, 53
Knights Templar 46
Knock, Ireland 30

Lang-Yang 61
Leo IX, Pope 59
Leo the Great, Pope 58
Litany of Loreto 66–7
Louis XI of France 53, 57
Lourdes, France 30, 93
Lucy 10
Luke 31, 55, **78**
Luther, Martin 23, 55, 64

Madeleine Sophie Barat 63
Marcellus 52
Margaret of Antioch 51, 54
Margaret of Scotland 57
Maria Goretti 43
Maria Teresa Ledóchowska 33
Mark **77**
Martin of Tours 19, 23, 46, 53
martyrs 6, 10–11, 16, 17, 27, 29
    child martyrs 42
    Forty Martyrs 23
    martyrs of China 60–1
    missionaries 28
    Spanish Civil War 53
Mary Guo-Li 61
Mary Magdalene 55, **74**
Mary the Virgin see Blessed Virgin
Mary Tudor 27
Matthew 38, 40, **76**
Matthias 40
Maurists 47
Maximian, Emperor 52

Michael 52
Michael Cerularius 59
miracles 17, 18–19
missionaries 28–9
monastic orders 13, 15, 46–7
Moses 14
Mother Teresa of Calcutta 17, 32, **33**
music 55
mysticism 15, 33

New World 28–9
Nicetas of Remesiana 55
Nicholas of Myra 14
Notre-Dame, Chartres 64

Odile 19, 35
Olaf 56–7
Orthodox Church 6, 14–15, 55, 59, 67
    icons 15
Oswald 56
Our Lady of Czestochowa 19, 31
Our Lady of Walsingham 22, 23

Pachomius 13, 46
Padre Pio 31
Pantaleon 51
Paolo 61
papacy 16–17, 40
    saintly popes 58–9
patron saints 68–9
    nations 48–9
    professions 44–5
Paul 20, 22, 34, 58, 77, **83**
Paul Lang Fu 43
Paul Miki 28
Paul VI, Pope 23, 33
Pedro Sanz 60
Pelagia of Antioch 42
Peter 22, 40, 58, 77, **81**, 82
Peter Wu Guosheng 61
Philomena 17, 42
Pierre Toussaint 32–3
Pietà 54
pilgrimages 9, 21, 22–3, 30–1
Pius V, Pope 59
Pius X, Pope 59

Reformation 9, 23, 26–7, 47, 57
    art as idolatry 55
    church architecture 64–5
relics 20–1, 22–3
religious orders 46–7
reliquaries 21

rescues 19
Rita of Cascia 63
Roch 28, 85
Roman Empire 10–11
royal saints 56–7

Santiego de Compostela, Spain 30–1
Sebastian 10, 54
Sergius of Radonezh 15
shrines 9, 21, 22–3, 30–1
Shroud of Turin 23
Simeon the New Theologian 15
Simon of Trent 17
Sixtus II, Pope 58
Sixtus V, Pope 66
St Michel and St Gudule, Brussels 64
Stephen 10, **79**
Stephen of Hungary 53, 56
stigmata 19

Theodore 51
Theresa of Avila 7, **92**
Theresa of Lisieux 13, **94**
Thomas 75
Thomas Becket 22, 23
Trappists 47
True Cross 21

Urban V, Pope 21
Ursula 11, 84

Valentine 17
Venerable status 17
Vincent Liem 61
virgins 11
visions 18–19
Vitus 51
Vladimir of Kiev 53, 56

warrior saints 52–3
William of Norwich 17